A FIRE IN THE BONES

A Fire
in the Bones

★

*Reflections on African-American
Religious History*

★

ALBERT J. RABOTEAU

Beacon Press
Boston

Earlier versions of some of the chapters in this book first appeared in the following: "Praying the ABCs: Reflections upon Faith in History" in *Cross Currents*, the quarterly journal of the Association for Religion and Intellectual Life, Fall, 1992; "African-Americans, Exodus, and the American Israel" in *African-American Christianity: Essays in History*, ed. Paul E. Johnson, © 1994 The Regents of the University of California; "How Far the Promised Land?" in *Religion and the Life of the Nation*, ed. Rowland A. Sherrill, © 1990 by the Board of Trustees of the University of Illinois, used by permission of the University of Illinois Press; "Richard Allen and the African Church Movement" in *Black Leaders of the Nineteenth Century*, ed. Leon Litwack and August Meier, © 1988 by the Board of Trustees of the University of Illinois, used by permission of the University of Illinois Press; "The Black Church: Continuity within Change" in *Altered Landscapes: Christianity in America, 1935–1985*, ed. David W. Lotz with Donald W. Shriver, Jr., and John F. Wilson, William B. Eerdmans Publishing Company, 1989, used by permission of the publisher; "The Conversion Experience" in *God Struck Me Dead: Voices of Ex-Slaves*, ed. Clifton H. Johnson, The Pilgrim Press, 1993, used by permission of the publisher.

Beacon Press
25 Beacon Street
Boston, Massachusetts 02108-2892

Beacon Press books
are published under the auspices of
the Unitarian Universalist Association of Congregations.

99 98 97 96   8 7 6 5 4 3 2

Text design by Wesley B. Tanner, Passim Editions
Composition by Wilsted & Taylor

Library of Congress Cataloging-in-Publication Data

Raboteau, Albert J.
    A fire in the bones: reflections on African-American religious history
/ Albert J. Raboteau.
        p. cm.
    Includes bibliographical references and index.
    ISBN 0-8070-0932-6 (cloth)
    ISBN 0-8070-0933-4 (paper)
    1. Afro-Americans—Religion. 2. United States—Church
history. I. Title.
BR563.N4R24 1995
277.3'08'08996073—dc20   94-36887
                                                                CIP

Contents

Preface

WHEN I WAS TEN YEARS OLD, I went to sing in Europe with five other choirboys from my parish church, St. Thomas the Apostle, Ann Arbor, Michigan. We six were selected to sing in Rome at an international congress of boys' choirs. After singing at St. Peter's Basilica, we would travel to Paris to spend a week at the headquarters of the sponsoring organization, the Singers of the Wooden Cross. I was the only African-American in our group, and as we mingled with other choirs from around the world in St. Peter's square, European singers, who had rarely, if ever, seen a black person, routinely asked me to pose for a picture with them. I agreed, rejecting the advice of one of my fellow Americans to "charge them a buck a picture." In Paris we were greeted by the director of the French Singers of the Wooden Cross, a jovial monsignor, who asked me to sing a "Negro spiritual," which, he claimed, "we love." Embarrassed, I refused his request to sing "Swing Low, Sweet Chariot" or "Go Down, Moses," and was surprised to learn that he, and apparently other foreigners, knew of these songs, which my mother sometimes sang while doing dishes or when worries saddened her spirit. Already singled out, I was reluctant to draw any more attention to myself. I also felt a vague unease about exhibiting something of my people for the enjoyment of white folks. I was troubled by his request, my uneasiness enhanced by a sense that spirituals belonged, not to our Roman

Catholic choir's public repertoire, but to a more private and med-
itative place, reflecting my people's distinctive identity, an identity
that I already felt uncomfortable about exposing so far from home
and family. I had never before felt so American and so un-
American at the same time.

My bewilderment about the complex relationship of race, religion, and national identity was shared, I would learn later, by
many Americans, white and black. Within months of my European trip, the United States Supreme Court delivered its decision
in *Brown v. Board of Education*, catalyzing forces that would soon
push the nation into a period of sustained and tumultuous struggle
over the meaning of race and the legality of racial discrimination.
In retrospect, I realize that my interest in African-American history and religion, an interest that has dominated my teaching, research, and writing over the past two decades, originated in the
issues that erupted for me and for the nation in those years. The
essays collected in this book represent the result of my attempts
to understand the religious history of black Americans and to as-
certain what that particular history means for the nation as a
whole.

Most of the essays collected in this volume (seven of the eleven)
have been published previously; some are new; a few have circulated widely in photocopy. Students and colleagues convinced me
that gathering them in one place would make them more accessible. I hope that this collection may serve another purpose as well,
encouraging renewed discussion of the racial and religious history
of the nation as we move rapidly toward the end of the twentieth
century, a century dominated, as W. E. B. Du Bois predicted, by
the "problem of the color line." The long encounter of black and
white Americans, which began tragically under slavery and still
proceeds under the long shadow of the plantation, remains the
paradigmatic test of the national experiment.

I encourage the reader to imagine this book as a quilt stitched together of separate pieces that fit, I trust, into an overall pattern. Composed for different invitations and to fit different occasions, these essays vary in tone and theme, some are more "historical" some more "reflective." All have in common my attempt to be faithful to the voices of African-American narrators as I heard them speak through historical documents of various sorts about the meaning(s) of black experience in America. I am convinced that their voices convey a treasury of wisdom and humanity we stand in sore need of hearing.

I owe thanks to my colleague and friend David Wills for perceptive readings and wise counsel "as always," to my editor at Beacon, Deb Chasman, for proposing and gracefully nurturing this project, and to all those whose invitations prompted these essays.

In response to that French priest's invitation to sing "one of your people's spirituals," I belatedly offer *A Fire in the Bones*.

Prologue

Praying the ABCs:
Reflections on Faith in History

I N 1862, A TEACHER NAMED Harriet Ware attended a funeral
on one of the South Carolina sea islands. Ware, a white missionary,
was surprised by the ceremony that her black pupils, all of them
recently freed slaves, devised to observe the burial. "As we drew
near to the grave we heard all the children singing their A, B, C,
through and through again, as they stood waiting round the grave
for the rest to assemble. . . . Each child had his school-book or
picture-book . . . in his hand,—another proof that they consider
their lessons as in some sort religious exercises."[1] Like Ware, many
missionaries were impressed by the former slaves' "superstitious"
regard for schooling and amazed at the sacrifices they were willing
to make to obtain book learning despite the poverty, uncertainty,
and precariousness of their lives in the postbellum South. When
asked, the freedmen frequently explained that they wanted to
learn so that they could read the Bible for themselves. Reading and
writing, moreover, seemed all the more precious to a people long
denied access to literacy under severe penalty of law. In effect,
learning to read and write gave concrete meaning to the notion of
freedom and enabled them to test its actual extent.

The image of those former slave children praying their ABCs
reminded me of the long and difficult struggle of black Americans
since emancipation to achieve better schooling for their children

in hopes that education would help them overcome the oppressive legacy of slavery. I would like to use that same image as an emblem for the following reflections upon the relationship between faith and the academic life, in particular the relationship between faith and history. Today the faith of black Americans in education as a solution to the intractable racial inequality of our society is severely threatened. Despite the current temptation to despair, I still share the former slaves' hope that education can help to make us free.

NARRATIVE AND MEANING

In my experience as historian and believer, faith and the academic life exist in a dialectical relationship of affinity and challenge. My faith and my historical scholarship reinforce and criticize each other in a variety of ways. The first of these contrapuntal relations revolves around the human need for story, for explanation of the world and our place in it. History, simply put, consists in telling stories about the ways that people lived in the past. Historians, as distinct from chroniclers, construct narratives that try to reveal the meaning of past events.

Narration is of course already an act of interpretation. Events do not speak for themselves. In this very fundamental sense, history is based upon an act of faith, the faith that events are susceptible of meanings that can be described in narration. Historical narrative places a mythic structure upon events by the very act of arranging them in a sequence of meaning, with a beginning, a middle, and an end. Instead of viewing time as a random chaos of atomistic experience, history assumes that the past has structure, meaning, consequence.

Christian faith also asserts that the events of human experience have meaning, a coherent pattern, a *telos*. But the source of that meaning for the believer ultimately lies outside history in the will and providence of God. From this "perspective of eternity," the challenge of religious faith to the meaning of historical narratives may be formulated in several questions: How can you know what events or what characters are significant? How can you find a vantage point within history from which you can judge the significance of human events? And without such a vantage point, aren't your interpretations arbitrary and all too prone to the fallacy of presentism, that is, judging the significance of what happened in the past by reference to issues of particular significance in the present?

On the other hand, the challenge of history to faith is to demonstrate to believers the historicity of their religious doctrines and institutions. History mounts a powerful critique against any religion's tendency to present a triumphalist myth of itself as a timeless, universalist institution preserving an unchanging deposit of doctrine transcending time and disparate cultures. In this sense, history taken seriously reminds Christian believers of the scandal of the Incarnation, the historical specificity and contingency of Jesus and of the "Jesus movement" in its origins and subsequent development.[2] By emphasizing the facticity and distinctiveness of all times, places, and peoples, history promotes appreciation of their uniqueness.

History and religious faith coalesce for me in their mutual admission of the necessity of plot. Both present narrative constructions of reality. Both answer to the basic human drive for order. Both lead us to search for the "hidden wholeness" of life, the connectedness of apparently fragmented and chaotic bits of experience and knowledge.[3] Of course, the problem for the believer, and the historian as well, lies precisely in "reading the signs of the times," to put it in Christian terms. The history of history and the history of Christianity are replete with divergent and conflicting explanations of what events really mean. Examples spring readily to mind. Those of us old enough to remember the un-ecumenical church history of pre–Vatican II days may recall the historiographical battles over whether the breakup of Christendom in sixteenth-century Europe should be considered a "Protestant Reformation" or a "Protestant Revolt," and whether the ensuing response of the Church of Rome was a "Catholic Reformation" or a "Catholic Counter Reformation." Or consider the more timely controversy over the 500th anniversary of Cristóbal Colón's fateful landfall on an island called Guanahani by its Arawak inhabitants and San Salvador by the admiral. Was Columbus's voyage a discovery, an invasion, or an encounter? And from whose perspective? To take an example from my own work on the religious history of American slaves, one of the most fundamental interpretations of national history, repeated so long and so often that it has taken on the power of myth, is the image of America as a New Israel. This myth of national identity depicts the European migration across the Atlantic from the old world to the new as an escape from Egyptian bondage to the Promised Land of milk and honey. For African-Americans, however, the myth is inverted. For us, the Middle Passage was a voyage from freedom in Africa to perpetual bondage in an America that in biblical terms did not resemble Israel but Egypt. "Go down, Moses," sang these American slaves, appropriating the story of Exodus, "and tell ol' Pharaoh to let my people go." As the historian Vincent Harding has noted, it is an abiding and tragic irony of our national history that white America's claim to be a New Israel has been constantly denied by Old Israel still enslaved in her midst. Clearly these conflicting interpretations of the past are not simply questions of fact, resolvable by more historical research. They result from the fact that history has served in the past and still serves today to establish and legitimate the identities of various communities. The conflicting claims upon history made by the search of different communities for meaning raises the issue of whose story it is that history tells.

WHOSE HISTORY?

In my own field, for example, for too many years the dominant culture, academic as well as popular, ignored the presence or distorted the role of African-Americans in the nation's history. Black Americans, if historians discussed them at all, figured prominently only in the story of slavery and in the topic of race relations. In both cases, they appeared not as actors in the national drama but as victims or problems. As an oppressed minority, they represented an unfortunate but minor exception to the main plot of American history: the gradual expansion of democracy to include all citizens. A few countervailing voices protested the inaccuracy of this consensus version of our history, but in the main, black people and their culture remained absent from courses in American history down to the 1960s. We were, so to speak, invisible. And the results of invisibility were devastating. In the absence of black history, a myth of the American past developed, a myth that denied black people any past of significance. Implicitly, and sometimes explicitly, they were dismissed by major historians as mere imitators of white culture. When I informed faculty colleagues in the late 1960s that I was researching the religious life of blacks, the typical response was, "Weren't they all Baptists and Methodists?" In other words, "Weren't they just like white Baptists and Methodists, except for the color of their skin?"

Between the mid 1960s and the early 1970s, the prevailing myth about black history was called into question on campus after campus across the land, as cries of civil rights activists for black power and black pride roused students, black and white, to demand courses in African-American history and culture. Recognizing (sometimes under pressure) the cogency of these demands, administrators and faculty at significant numbers of schools added new courses and revised old ones to take into account the black experience. African-American studies departments mushroomed, and various programs in ethnic studies and eventually women's studies followed. The recovery of African-American history served as a paradigm for the recovery of the pasts of other peoples whose stories had also been left out of American history.

This shift in perspective has affected religious as well as secular history. No longer is it responsible for students of American religious history to ignore the religious experience of black Americans, or that of other people of color, or of women, as if they were invisible. If the history of religion in America is the subject, then it should include the religious life of all the peoples who make up America, not just the religion of white Protestant males.

The inclusion of African-Americans and other previously invisible groups in the history books is an extremely important development not just for academic study but for our understanding of American society and ultimately our understanding of ourselves, for history functions as a form of self-definition. In its pages we read ourselves. It tells us who we are because it reveals where we come from and where we've been. History, especially religious history, because it touches on the deepest myths, beliefs, and values of our society, is important to each of us. To change our view of history changes our view of ourselves. The current debate about multiculturalism is precisely about this issue of redefinition. Those left out of the history books are insisting that they be included, but they also demand more than mere inclusion. They want to change the very plot of the story. Ralph Ellison's wise and funny novel *The Invisible Man* contains an episode that brilliantly illustrates the significance of including these "others" in the national story. The novel's unnamed protagonist finds a job working in a factory for Liberty Paints, a company that makes an extremely profitable product called Optic White, a paint widely used to whitewash government buildings, churches, and national monuments. Ironically, the secret formula for mixing Optic White is known by one person in the factory, an old black janitor who works in a subbasement deep below the plant. The closely guarded secret lies in the exact calibration of ten black drops added to the paint base. If just the right amount is not added, the paint will turn out gray or brown, not Optic White. Similarly, the challenge of black history, ethnic history, and women's history is not simply to furnish the additional drops necessary to continue the whitewash of our national experience. The predominant theme of American history has often, for example, been presented as the gradual spread of democracy to more and more people. And to some extent that has been true. But as Edmund Morgan, a historian of colonial America, has pointed out, there is another plot line that is just as accurate, the continued enslavement and oppression of black Americans. Moreover, argues Morgan, the two themes are so intertwined that the story of America should be seen as the progression of an ongoing paradox, the paradox of American freedom and American slavery.[4]

Over the past two decades, historians have come to realize that if history is to be an adequate story of people who lived in the past, it needs to tell the stories of all. It is not enough to concentrate upon elites or upon the exercise of power, upon wars and generals, or for that matter, councils and bishops. Moreover, the need to be inclusive calls into question the privileging of any one group or people as the standard of measure. The mythmaking uses to which history is put can indeed be dangerous. Here Christianity, with its claims to universality, offers a useful challenge to history as communal myth, questioning the temptation to turn the past into a jingoistic celebration of ethnic or national superiority. Conversely, the challenge of history to Christianity entails a critique of its tendency to reduce theology to a monolithic ideology and its transformation of missionary zeal into imperialism. Christianity has all too often validated what Martin Luther King, Jr., called "the deadly arrogance of the West" and cloaked the brutality of conquest under the mantle of preaching the gospel. Examples could easily be multiplied, but permit me to mention one of particular significance to my work.

From the inception of the Atlantic slave trade, conversion of the slaves to Christianity was viewed by European Christians as a justification for the enslavement of Africans. When Portuguese adventurers returned from West Africa with slaves in the mid-fifteenth century, Gomes Eannes de Zurara, the court chronicler, noted their achievements and observed that "the greater benefit" belonged not to the Portuguese but to the captive Africans, "for though their bodies were now brought into some subjection, that was a small matter in comparison of their souls, which would now possess true freedom for evermore."[5] Zurara, who witnessed the brutal separation and sale of a group of captive Africans and was moved to tears by the event, later repented that his emotions had gotten the better of his Christian conscience, because the slaves would receive the benefits of civilization and Christianity. Zurara's rationalization was repeated for more than four centuries by successive generations of Christian apologists for slavery. Certainly there were some exceptions, such as the justly celebrated Fray Bartolomé de las Casas, whose defense of the full humanity of the Indians still stirs readers with moral indignation, but the long history of atrocities committed in the name of the gospel requires of believers not excuses but acceptance, reflection, and repentance. History and faith prompt each other to extend the sense of community to include the powerless, the poor, the weak, the inarticulate and to make present the invisible, those left out or ignored as pejorative others. They also encourage a great deal of modesty about the role of one's own community in history, whether conceived as the history of civilization or the history of salvation.

TRAVELING ABROAD, TRAVELING WITHIN

To quote the title of David Lowenthal's 1985 book, the past is a foreign country. The people who lived in the past were by that very fact different, and respecting them as people requires that we understand their differences from us, in part so that we can better understand our own character and situation. To do so requires imagination and empathy. Studying other times and places is like a journey, whose purpose is not only to interest but also to change the traveler. Like literature, history has the capacity to expand our vision of human lives and cultures. History also demonstrates the limitations of one's own culture, its values, assumptions, and beliefs. To familiarize the alien and to alienate the familiar is one of the basic purposes of education. History is one of the academic disciplines most likely to inspire students to question their received values, religious and cultural, by showing them that there are others, some of which conflict with their own. This historical challenge to accepted values can lead to a crisis of faith among believers as they encounter cogent alternatives to their own beliefs. The very fact of pluralistic alternatives may lead some to adopt relativism. The same questioning, however, may also make it possible for believers to mature in faith, by presenting them an opportunity to choose among alternate belief systems and commit themselves to a set of values, thus "owning" the religious culture in which they were raised. History offers us a salutary reminder that part of faith is doubt.

Conversely, faith challenges history to take seriously the religious beliefs and practices in which people of the past gave meaning and value to their lives. From the perspective of faith, the attempt of some historians to locate religion as a mere midway station in the evolution of cultures from the stage of magic to the stage of science demonstrates an inadequate grasp of religion and a simplistic understanding of history. Moreover, faith cautions history against reducing religion to an epiphenomenon of economic or political ideology. It is not that economic and political concerns play no role in religion. But the existential dimensions of religion as resources for people facing the perennial questions of the human condition, questions of meaning raised by suffering, sickness, and death, require deeper reflection and more sensitive analysis.

In my imaginary dialogue, faith and history acknowledge the truth of the adage "One person's superstition is another person's religion" and agree to make an effort to understand the beliefs of others, no matter how strange they seem to be. Having reached agreement in principle, the historian asks the believer, Why do Christians demonize the religious practices of others that at base seem so similar to their own? The believer turns to the historian and asks, Why do historians romanticize the religions of other cultures while reflecting bias toward the Christianity of their own?

Ultimately, I believe that the historical journey helps to transform us by enabling us to understand the "others" and in understanding them come to a deeper understanding of ourselves. The theologian John Dunne has aptly called the process I'm describing as "passing over and returning home," the journey to self-knowledge through empathetic intuition (admittedly imperfect and vicarious) of the experience of others. In this journey, we encounter difference not as something alienating but as simply different. If that goal sounds jejune, one has only to survey the history of encounters between foreign cultures around the world to realize how rare it actually is. Ideally, the journey I am envisaging leads not only to knowledge but to compassion. Faith confirms and completes the experience by reminding us that there are no aliens, no others, but only sisters and brothers.

"LOVE OF LEARNING AND THE DESIRE FOR GOD"
There is another sense in which I think history, or more broadly speaking, the academic life, can transform persons.[6] Despite the bureaucracy of our institutions of higher learning, they still offer space for nurturing the love of learning, the free play of curiosity, the pursuit of knowledge for its own sake—in a word, the intellectual life. A respite from exclusive preoccupation with "getting and spending," the academy still supports the fundamental principle that "the unexamined life is not worth living." Implicit in dedication to the life of the mind is a critique of materialism.

Moreover, the academy attempts to infect students with the lifelong virus of learning. College, we fondly and probably foolishly hope, is just the beginning of a passion for learning. We like to think we teach disciplines, in the double sense of a subject and a habit of mind—a way of critical thinking. Discipline also describes the demands made upon us by that hard taskmaster, research. Often lonely, difficult, tedious work, historical research can involve months and years of searching in dusty archives through mountains of manuscript and printed sources for the nuggets of information that go into reconstructing a glimpse of the past. Delayed gratification is an apt description of a good deal of the research experience.

Obviously, I am describing an ideal (shaped no doubt by my own education in the liberal arts curriculum of a Jesuit university), and yet I think the ideal describes values that we in the academy lose at the peril of our souls. Here, too, I find the dialogue between my faith and my academic life a helpful corrective. Faith criticizes the university for failing to nurture the life of the mind. It condemns the rampant commodification of knowledge as simply another instance of mammon worship cloaked in the garb of advancing knowledge. Faith decries the self-aggrandizing instinct of scholars who take a proprietary attitude toward their fields of expertise. Faith asks whether the notion of a community of scholars has any basis in reality on campuses today, or whether it simply masks one more aggregate of consumers, wandering in a market place of ideas.

In turn, the academy examines the churches and too often finds them intellectually wanting. The life of the spirit cannot ignore the life of the mind. Fideism and anti-intellectualism diminish both mind and spirit and squander the rich Christian heritage of "faith seeking understanding." The churches and Christian scholars need to revitalize the ideal of the intellectual life as a vocation and hold it up as a worthy model for the young. We need, moreover, to reappropriate in our own day the tradition of Christian spirituality, which teaches us that the life of faith and the life of the mind ultimately come together in pursuit of wisdom. Wisdom, according to this tradition, strips us of illusions and of false ambitions, freeing us to perceive with single-minded clarity what spiritual masters have long understood, that the insatiable desire of the human spirit for knowledge is an expression of our profound yearning for the infinite reality of God.

SALVATION HISTORY

The Christian believes that God acts in history, though the how and when remain a mystery. In my study of African-American history, I have been moved by the pervasive faith of black Christians that God was acting in their own history. Adopting the biblical image of a God who lifts up and casts down nations, black Christians warned antebellum America (in terms strikingly prophetic of the Civil War) that it stood in peril of divine judgment unless it quickly repented the sin of slavery (an interpretation belatedly shared by Lincoln). And Christian slaves appropriated the story of Exodus as prefiguring their own history of bondage and future deliverance. The sacred history of God's liberation of his people would be reenacted in the American South. In times of despair, they repeated the story of Exodus and took hope. As a slave named Polly eloquently explained to her mistress: "We poor creatures have need to believe in God, for if God Almighty will not be good to us some day, why were we born? When I heard of his delivering his people from bondage. I know it means the poor Africans."[7]

The coming of the Civil War and Emancipation validated the slave's belief that God acts in human history. "Shout the glad tidings o'er Egypt's dark sea / Jehovah has triumphed, his people are free!" they sang. But it did not take long for the freedmen to learn that though slavery had ended, its legacy of oppression remained. During the last decades of the nineteenth century, the situation of black Americans seemed to worsen, not improve, as lynchings mounted to epidemic proportion; as black voters were disfranchised by intimidation, violence, or legal subterfuge; as Jim Crow laws spread across the South and separate but equal became the law of the land in the *Plessy v. Ferguson* decision of 1896; as new forms of pseudoscientific racism depicted the Negro as a beast or, alternately, a child. Internationally the "scramble for Africa" parceled out the "dark continent" among rival European powers, while the United States shouldered its own white man's burden in the far-off Philippines. It is no wonder that historians of black America label this period "the nadir."[8]

Faced with the question of meaning and the necessity of staving off despair, several black clergymen articulated a theology of history in which they lambasted American Christians for turning Christianity into a clan religion. Condemning the jingoism of the age, they accused Americans of worshiping Anglo-Saxonism instead of Christ. It was impossible for America to civilize and to evangelize the world because civilization, moving ever westward, had finally washed up on these shores spent of all its force. America had been displaced in God's plan of salvation and it would be the mission of the "darker races of the world" to finally put into practice the gospel, which Europeans and Americans had only managed to preach. The darker races would develop a classless, raceless, and weaponless Christianity that would welcome the return of the Universal Christ. In this theology of history, it was the destiny of those who had been oppressed, who had been hated, who had been rejected, but who had not oppressed, hated, or rejected in return, to bring salvation to the world.

It was, then, an old tradition that Martin Luther King, Jr., drew upon in enunciating the concept of redemptive suffering. He learned it from the preaching of his father and his grandfather in the pulpit of Ebenezer Baptist Church in Atlanta; he learned it from the hymns sung by the choir—a tradition recognized by Gandhi himself, who remarked to Howard and Sue Bailey Thurman that the spiritual "Were You There When They Crucified My Lord" got to "the root of the experience of the entire human race under the spread of the healing wings of suffering."[9] In this historical reading, the black American experience represented the experience of those who suffer anywhere.

The historian as historian remains agnostic about such claims—they cannot be validated or invalidated by historical research. And yet, I, as historian and believer, cannot but hope that our history is touched by the providence of God. Faced with the mystery of discerning God's design in history, I find myself returning to the company of those former slave children, praying their ABCs.

Part I

In Search of the Promised Land

*African-American Religion
and American Destiny*

Chapter One

African-Americans, Exodus, and the American Israel

Canaan land is the land for me,
And let God's saints come in.
There was a wicked man,
He kept them children in Egypt land.
Canaan land is the land for me,
And let God's saints come in.
God did say to Moses one day,
Say, Moses, go to Egypt land,
And tell him to let my people go.
Canaan land is the land for me,
And let God's saints come in.

Slave spiritual

IN THE ENCOUNTER WITH European Christianity in its Protestant form in North America, enslaved Africans and their descendants were exposed to something new: a fully articulated ritual relationship with the Supreme Being, who was pictured in the book that the Christians called the Bible not just as the Creator and Ruler of the Cosmos, but as the God of History, a God who lifted up and cast down nations and peoples, a God whose sovereign will was directing all things toward an ultimate end, drawing good out of evil. As they reflected upon the evil that had befallen them and their parents, they increasingly turned to the language, symbols, and world view of the Christian Holy Book. There they found a theology of history that helped them to make sense out of

17

their enslavement. One story in particular caught their attention and fascinated them with its implications and potential applications to their own situation. That story was the story of Exodus. What they did with that ancient story of the Near East is the topic of this essay.

CONVERSION

From the beginning of the Atlantic slave trade, Europeans claimed that the conversion of slaves to Christianity justified the enslavement of Africans. Yet the conversion of slaves was not a high priority for colonial planters. British colonists in North America proved especially indifferent, if not downright hostile, to the conversion of their slaves. At first, opposition was based on the suspicion that English law forbade the enslavement of Christians and so would require slaveholders to emancipate any slave who received baptism. Masters suspected that slaves would therefore seek to be baptized in order to gain freedom. These fears were quickly allayed by colonial legislation declaring that baptism did not alter slave status.

With the legal obstacles aside, slaveowners for the most part still demonstrated scant interest in converting their slaves. According to the common wisdom, Christianity spoiled slaves. Christian slaves thought too highly of themselves, became impudent, and even turned rebellious. Moreover, Anglo-Americans were troubled by a deep-seated uneasiness at the prospect of a slave's claiming Christian fellowship with white people. Africans were foreign; to convert them was to make them more like the English and therefore deserving of better treatment. In fact, religion, like language and skin color, constituted the colonist's identity. To Christianize black-skinned Africans, therefore, would confuse the distinctiveness of the races and threaten the social order based upon that distinctiveness. Finally, the labor, not the souls of the slaves, concerned most slaveholders. Peter Kalm, a Swedish traveler in America from 1748 to 1750, perceptively described the colonists' objections to religious instruction for slaves:

> It is . . . to be pitied, that the masters of these negroes in most of the English colonies take little care of their spiritual welfare, and let them live on in their Pagan darkness. There are even some, who would be very ill pleased at, and would by all means hinder their negroes from being instructed in the doctrines of Christianity; to this they are partly led by the conceit of its being shameful, to have a spiritual brother or sister among so despicable a people; partly by thinking that they should not be able to keep their negroes so meanly afterwards; and partly through fear of the negroes growing too proud, on seeing themselves upon a level with their masters in religious matters.[1]

A concerted attack on these obstacles to slave conversion was mounted by the Church of England in 1701 when it established the Society for the Propagation of the Gospel in Foreign Parts to support missionaries to the colonies. The society's first task was to convince masters that they had a duty to instruct their slaves in the truths of the gospel. In tract after tract, widely distributed in the colonies, officers of the society stressed the compatibility of Christianity with slavery. Masters need not fear that religion would ruin their slaves. On the contrary, Christianity would make them better slaves by convincing them to obey their owners out of a sense of moral duty instead of out of fear. After all, society pamphlets explained, Christianity does not upset the social order, but supports it: "Scripture, far from making an alteration in Civil Rights, expressly directs that every man abide in the condition wherein he is called, with great indifference of mind concerning outward circumstances."[2] To prove the point, such tracts reiterated ad nauseam the verse from Ephesians 6:5: "Slaves be obedient to your masters." The missionaries thus denied that spiritual equality implied worldly equality; they restricted the egalitarian impulse of Christianity to the realm of the spirit. So, in effect, they built a religious foundation to support slavery. As the historian Winthrop Jordan aptly put it, "These clergymen had been forced by the circumstance of racial slavery in America into propagating the Gospel by presenting it as an attractive device for slave control."[3]

The success of missions to the slaves depended largely on circumstances beyond the missionaries' control: the proportion of African-born to Creole slaves, the geographic location and work patterns of the slaves, and the ratio of blacks to whites in a given locale. Blacks in the North and in the Chesapeake region of Maryland and Virginia, for example, experienced more frequent and closer contact with whites than did those of the lowland coasts of South Carolina and Georgia, where large gangs of African slaves toiled on isolated rice plantations with only limited and infrequent exposure to whites or their religion. Even if a missionary gained regular access to slaves, the slaves did not invariably accept the Christian gospel. Some rejected it, according to missionary accounts, because of "the Fondness they have for their old Heathenish Rites, and the strong Prejudice they must have against Teachers from among those, whom they serve so unwillingly."[4] Others accepted Christianity because they hoped—colonial legislation and missionary pronouncements notwithstanding—that baptism would raise their status and ensure eventual freedom for their children, if not for themselves. One missionary in South Carolina required slaves seeking baptism to swear an oath that they did not request the sacrament out of a desire for freedom. (Apparently he missed the irony.) Missionaries complained that, even after instruction and baptism, slaves still mixed Christian beliefs with the traditional practices of their African homelands.

Discouraging though the prospects were, colonial clergymen had established a few successful missions among the slaves by the early eighteenth century. When the bishop of London distributed a list of questions in 1724 requiring ministers to describe their work among the slaves, several respondents reported impressive numbers of baptisms. The great majority, however, stated vague intentions instead of concrete achievements. During the first 120 years of black slavery in British North America, Christianity made little headway in the slave population.

Slaves were first converted in large numbers in the wake of the religious revivals that periodically swept parts of the colonies beginning in the 1740s. Accounts by George Whitefield, Gilbert Tennent, Jonathan Edwards, and other revivalists made special mention of the fact that blacks were flocking to hear the message of salvation in hitherto unseen numbers. Not only were free blacks and slaves attending revivals, but they were also taking active part in the services as exhorters and preachers. For a variety of reasons, Evangelical revivalists succeeded where Anglican missionaries had failed. Whereas the Anglicans had depended upon a slow process of indoctrination, the Evangelicals preached the immediate experience of conversion as the primary requirement for baptism, thereby making Christianity more accessible. Because of the centrality of the conversion experience in their piety, Evangelicals tended to deemphasize instruction and downplay learning as prerequisites of Christian life. As a result, all classes of society were welcome to participate actively in prayer meetings and revival services, in which the poor, the illiterate, and even the enslaved prayed, exhorted, and preached.

After the Revolution, revival fervor continued to flare up sporadically in the South. More and more slaves converted to Christianity under the dramatic preaching of Evangelical revivalists, especially Methodists and Baptists. The emotionalism of the revivals encouraged the outward expression of religious feeling, and the sight of black and white converts weeping, shouting, fainting, and moving in ecstatic trance became a familiar, if sensationalized, feature of the sacramental and camp meeting seasons. In this heated atmosphere, slaves found a form of Christian worship that resembled the religious celebrations of their African heritage. The analogy between African and Evangelical styles of worship enabled the slaves to reinterpret the new religion by reference to the old, and so made this brand of Christianity seem less foreign than that of the more liturgically sedate Church of England.

The rise of the Evangelical denominations, particularly the Methodists and the Baptists, threatened the established Anglican church in the South. Appealing to the "lower sort," the Evangelicals suffered persecution at the hands of the Anglican authorities. Baptist preachers were jailed, their services were disrupted, and in Virginia, they were roughed up by rowdies who thought it humorous to immerse the Baptists in mud. They were thought of as different in an unsettling sort of way. "There was a company of them in the back part of our town, and an outlandish set of people they certainly were," remarked one woman to the early Baptists' historian David Benedict. "You yourself would say so if you had seen them. . . . You could hardly find one among them but was deformed in some way or other."[5]

The Evangelicals seemed to threaten the social as well as the religious order by accepting slaves into their societies and conventicles. An anti-Baptist petition warned the Virginia assembly in 1777 that "there have been nightly meetings of slaves to receive the instruction of these teachers without the consent of their masters, which have produced very bad consequences."[6] In the 1780s the Evangelicals' challenge to the social order became explicit. Methodist conferences in 1780, 1783, and again in 1784 strongly condemned slavery and tried "to extirpate this abomination," first from the ministry and then from the membership as a whole, by passing increasingly stringent regulations against slaveowning, slave-buying, and slave-selling. Several Baptist leaders freed their slaves, and in 1789 the General Committee of Virginia Baptists condemned slavery as "a violent deprivation of the rights of nature."[7]

In the South, these antislavery moves met with strong, immediate, and, as the leadership quickly realized, irreversible opposition. In 1785, the Baltimore Conference of the Methodist Church suspended the rule against slavery. Methodist leader Thomas Coke explained, "We thought it prudent to suspend the minute concerning slavery, on account of the great opposition that had been given it, our work being in too infantile a state to push things to extremity."[8] Local Baptist associations in Virginia responded to the General Committee's attack on slavery by declaring that the subject was "so abstruse" that no religious society had the right to concern itself with the issue as a society. Each individual should be left "to act at discretion in order to keep a good conscience before God, as far as the laws of our land will admit."[9] As for the slaves, the goal of the church should be the amelioration of their treatment, not emancipation.

Thus, the Evangelical challenge to slavery in the late eighteenth century failed. The intransigence of slavery once again set the limits of the Christian egalitarian impulse just as it had in the days of the colonial Anglican mission. Rapid growth of the Baptist and Methodist churches, rather than overthrowing slavery, instead forced an ineluctable accommodation to slaveholding principles. At the beginning of the nineteenth century, Robert Semple, another Baptist historian, described the change that had come over the "outlandish" Baptists after 1790:

> Their preachers became much more correct in their manner of preaching. A great many odd tones, disgusting whoops and awkward gestures were disused. . . . Their zeal was less mixed with enthusiasm, and their piety became more rational. They were much more numerous, and, of course, in the eyes of the world, more respectable. Besides, they were joined by persons of much

greater weight in civil society; their congregations became more numerous. . . . This could not but influence their manners and spirit more or less.[10]

Though both Methodists and Baptists rapidly retreated from antislavery pronouncements, their struggle with the established order and their uneasiness about slavery gave slaves, initially at least, the impression that they were "friendly toward freedom." For a short time, revivalistic Evangelicalism breached the wall that colonial missionaries had built between spiritual and temporal equality. Clearly, converting slaves to Christianity could have more than spiritual implications, a possibility slaves were eager to explore.

Methodists and Baptists backed away from these implications in the 1790s, but they had already taken a momentous step, and it proved to be irreversible. Thanks to the willingness of the Evangelical churches to license black men to exhort and preach, a significant group of black preachers had begun during the 1770s and 1780s to pastor their own people. Mainly Baptist, since the congregational independence of the Baptists gave them more leeway to preach than any other denomination, much of their ministry was informal and extraecclesial. It would be difficult to overestimate the importance of these early black preachers for the development of an African-American Christianity. In effect, they mediated between Christianity and the experience of the slaves (and free blacks), interpreting the stories, symbols, and events of the Bible to fit the day-to-day lives of those held in bondage. And whites—try as they might—could not determine the "accuracy" of this interpretation. Nurturing Christian communities among slaves and free blacks, these pioneer preachers began to build an independent black church in the last quarter of the eighteenth century. Slave preachers, exhorters, and church-appointed watchmen instructed their fellow slaves, nurtured their religious development, and brought them to conversion, in some cases without the active involvement of white missionaries or masters at all. The spread of Baptist and Methodist Evangelicalism between 1770 and 1820 changed the religious complexion of the South by bringing unprecedented numbers of slaves into membership in the Church and by introducing even larger numbers to at least the rudiments of Christianity. During the antebellum decades, Christianity diffused through the slave quarters, though most slaves did not hold membership in regular churches. Those slaves who did attend church generally attended with whites, but some, more than historians have realized, attended separate black churches.

We tend to identify the development of the independent black church with free blacks in the North, but the same spirit of religious independence also created separate black churches in the South. Several "African" churches, as they were called, sprang up before 1800. Some of these black congregations were independent to the extent that they called their own pastors and officers, joined local associations with white churches, and sent their own delegates to associational meetings. This early independence of black preachers and churches was curtailed during the antebellum period, particularly in reaction to slave conspiracies, when all gatherings of blacks for whatever purpose were viewed with alarm. For slaves to participate in the organization, leadership, and governance of church structures was perceived as dangerous. Nevertheless, black churches continued to grow in size and number, strange as it may seem, in the slave South. Though nominally controlled by whites, these separate congregations were frequently led by black ministers, some free, and some slave. Often, they outnumbered the largest white churches in the local church associations. Never numerous in the South, the separate black churches were extremely important, if limited, institutional expressions of black religious independence from white control.

In the North, the abolition of slavery after the Revolution gave black congregations and clergy much more control over their religious lives. Federal and state disestablishment of religion created an environment of voluntarism in which church organization flourished. Between 1790 and 1820, black Episcopalians, black Methodists, black Baptists, and black Presbyterians founded churches, exercised congregational control where possible, and struggled with white elders, bishops, and associations to gain autonomy. Among the first to do so was Bethel African Methodist Episcopal (AME) Church in Philadelphia. Founded in 1794 by Richard Allen, a former slave who had become a licensed Methodist preacher, Bethel was organized after discriminatory treatment drove black Methodists to abandon St. George's, the white church they had supported for years. Two other African Methodist denominations had organized by 1821. Though the black Methodists were the first to take independent control of their church property, finances, and governance on the denominational level, northern blacks in other churches demonstrated their spirit of independence as well. These black churches not only formed the institutional core for the development of free black communities, they also gave black Christians the opportunity to articulate publicly their own vision of Christianity, standing in eloquent testimony to the existence of two Christian Americas.

Of course, independent religious institutions were out of the question for the vast majority of black Americans, suffering the system of slavery in the southern states. They attended church, if they attended at all, with whites or under white supervision. Nevertheless, slaves developed their own "invisible institution" of extraecclesial religious life. In the slave quarters and brush arbors, they held their own religious meetings where they interpreted Christianity according to their experience and, conversely, interpreted their experience by means of the myths, stories, and symbols of Christianity. They were even willing to risk severe punishment to attend forbidden prayer meetings in order to worship God free of white control. A former slave, Lucretia Alexander, explained why:

The preacher came and . . . he'd just say, "Serve your masters. Don't steal your master's turkey. Don't steal your master's chickens. Don't steal your master's hawgs. Don't steal your master's meat. Do whatsomever your master tell you to do." Same old thing all the time. My father would have church in dwelling houses and they had to whisper. . . . Sometimes they would have church at his house. That would be when they want a real meetin' with some real preachin'. . . . They used to sing their songs in a whisper. That was a prayer meeting from house to house . . . once or twice a week.[11]

Inevitably, the slaves' Christianity contradicted that of their masters, for the slaves knew that no matter how sincerely religious a slaveowner might be, his Christianity was compatible with slavery, and theirs was not. The division went deep; it extended to the fundamental interpretation of the Bible. The dichotomy between the faiths of black and white Christians was described by a white Methodist minister who pastored a black congregation in Charleston, South Carolina, in 1862:

There were near fourteen hundred colored communicants. . . . [Their] service was always thronged—galleries, lower floor, chancel, pulpit, steps and all. . . . The preacher could not complain of any deadly space between himself and his congregation. He was positively breast up to his people, with no possible loss of . . . rapport. Though ignorant of it at the time, he remembers now the cause of the enthusiasm under his deliverances [about] the "law of liberty" and "freedom from Egyptian bondage." What was figurative they interpreted literally. He thought of but one ending of the war; they quite another. He remembers the sixty-eighth Psalm as affording numerous texts for their delectation, e.g., "Let God arise, let his enemies be scattered"; His "march through the wilderness"; "The Chariots of God are twenty thousand"; "The hill of God is as the hill of Basham"; and especially, "Though ye have lain among the pots, yet shall ye be as the wings of a dove covered with silver, and her feathers with yellow gold." . . . It is mortifying now to think that his comprehension was not equal to the African intellect. All he thought about was relief from the servitude of sin, and freedom from the bondage of the devil. . . . But they interpreted it literally in the good time coming, which of course could not but make their ebony complexion attractive, very.[12]

What the preacher was describing was the end of a long process, spanning almost two hundred and fifty years, by which slaves came to accept the gospel of Christianity. But the slaves did not simply become Christians; they fashioned Christianity to fit their own peculiar experience of enslavement in America. The preacher, like many white Christians before and since, thought there was no distance between him and his "people," no possible loss of rapport. He learned belatedly that the chasm was wide and deep. As one freedman succinctly stated: "We couldn't tell NO PREACHER NEBER how we suffer all dese long years. He know'd nothin' 'bout we."[13]

EXODUS

No single story captures more clearly the distinctiveness of African-American Christianity than that of the Exodus. From the earliest days of colonization, white Christians had represented their journey across the Atlantic to America as the exodus of a New Israel; slaves identified themselves as the Old Israel, suffering bondage under a new Pharaoh. White American preachers, politicians, and other orators found in the story of Exodus a rich source of metaphors to explicate the unfolding history of the nation. Each section of the narrative—bondage in Egypt, rescue at the Red Sea, wandering in the wilderness, and entrance into the Promised Land—provided a typological map to reconnoiter the moral terrain of American society. John Winthrop, the leader of the great Puritan expedition to Massachusetts Bay Colony, set the pattern in his famous "Modell of Christian Charity" sermon composed on board ship in 1630. Having elaborated the settlers' covenantal obligations to God, echoing the Sinaitic covenant of Israel with Yahweh, Winthrop concluded his discourse with a close paraphrase of Moses' farewell instruction to Israel (Deuteronomy 30):

> Beloved there is now sett before us life, and good, deathe and evill in that wee are Commaunded this day to love the Lord our God, and to love one another, to walke in his wayes and to keepe his Commaundements and his Ordinance, and his lawes, and the Articles of our Covenant with him that wee may live and be multiplied, and that the Lord our God may blesse us in the land whither we goe to possess it: But if our heartes shall turne away soe that wee will not obey, but shall be seduced and worship . . . other Gods, our pleasures, and proffitts, and serve them; it is propounded unto this day, wee shall surely perishe out of the good Land whither wee passe over this vast Sea to possesse it.[14]

Notice the particular application that Winthrop draws from the Exodus story: possession of the land is contingent upon observing the moral obligations of the convenant with God. It is a mark of the greatness of Winthrop's address that the obligations he emphasizes are justice, mercy, affection, meekness, gentleness, patience, generosity, and unity—not the qualities usually associated with taking or keeping possession of a land. Later and lesser sermons would extol much more aggressive virtues. But even in Winthrop's address, there is an explicit notion of reciprocity between God's will and American destiny: "God has made a contract with us. If we live up to our part of the bargain, so will he." The idea of reciprocity between divine providence and America's destiny had tremendous hortatory power, and Puritan preachers exploited it to the full over the next century and more in the jeremiad. In sermon after sermon, a succession of New England divines deciphered droughts, epidemics, Indian attacks, and other misfortunes as tokens of God's displeasure over the sins of the nation. Unless people took the opportunity to humble themselves, repent, and reform, they might expect much more of the same. Implicit, however, in this understanding was the danger of seeing the will of God in the actions of America's settlers. Winthrop was too good a Puritan to succumb to this temptation. Protected by his belief in the total sovereignty of God, he knew that the relationship between God's will and human action was one-sided and that the proper human attitude was trust in God, not confidence in man. God's will was the measure of America's deeds, not vice versa. Of course, no American preacher or politician would have disagreed, but as time went on the salient features of the Exodus story changed. The farther Americans moved from the precariousness of Egypt toward the security of the Promised Land, the greater the danger of relaxing the tension between America's destiny and God's will.

The change is clear when we compare the tone of Winthrop's "Modell of Christian Charity" with that of an election sermon entitled "The United States Elevated to Glory and Honor," preached by Ezra Stiles in 1783. Flushed with excitement over the success of the Revolution, Stiles dwelled at length on the unfolding destiny of the new nation. Quoting, like Winthrop, from the book of Deuteronomy, Stiles struck a celebratory rather than a hortatory note:

> "And to make thee high above all nations which he hath made, in praise, and in name, and in honour; and that thou mayest be an holy people unto the Lord thy God." . . . I have assumed [this] text as introductory to a discourse upon the political welfare of God's American Israel, and as allusively prophetic of the future prosperity and splendour of the United States. . . . Already does the new constellation of the United States begin to realize this glory. It has already risen to an acknowledged sovereignty among the republicks and kingdoms of the world. And we have reason to hope, and I believe to expect, that God has still greater blessings in store for this vine which his own right hand hath planted, to make us "high among the nations in praise, and in name, and in honour."[15]

Stiles went on at great length to identify the reasons for his optimism about America's present and future preeminence, including the fact that "in our civil constitutions, those impediments are removed which obstruct the progress of society towards perfection." It's a long way from Winthrop's caution to Stiles's confidence, from an "Errand in the Wilderness" to "progress towards perfection." In Stiles's election sermon we can perceive God's New Israel becoming the Redeemer Nation. The destiny of New Israel was to reach the pinnacle of perfection and to carry liberty and the gospel around the globe. In tandem with this exaggerated vision of American destiny came an exaggerated vision of human capacity. In an increasingly confident and prosperous nation, it was difficult to avoid shifting the emphasis from divine sovereignty to human ability. Historian Conrad Cherry has succinctly summarized the change in perception of American destiny: "Believing that she had escaped the wickedness of the Old World and the guilt of the past, God's New Israel would find it all too easy to ignore her vices and all too difficult to admit a loss of innocence."[16] Except for the presence of another, a darker, Israel:

> America, America, foul and indelible is thy stain! Dark and dismal is the cloud that hangs over thee, for thy cruel wrongs and injuries to the fallen sons of Africa. The blood of her murdered ones cries to heaven for vengeance against Thee. . . . You may kill, tyrannize, and oppress as much as you choose, until our cry shall come up before the throne of God; for I am firmly persuaded, that he will not suffer you to quell the proud, fearless and undaunted spirits of the Africans forever; for in his own time, he is able to plead our cause against you, and to pour out upon you the ten plagues of Egypt.[17]

So wrote Maria Stewart, a free black reform activist in Boston during the 1830s. These words, written in 1831, were addressed to an America that projected itself as the probable site of the coming millennium, Christ's thousand-year reign of peace and justice. Slaves and free blacks like Maria Stewart located themselves in a different part of the Exodus story than white Christians. From their perspective America was Egypt, and as long as it continued to enslave and oppress black Israel, America's destiny was in jeopardy. America stood under the judgment of God, and unless it repented, the death and destruction visited upon biblical Egypt would be repeated here. The retribution envisaged was quite literal, as Mary Livermore, a white governess, discovered when she overheard a prayer uttered by Aggy, the housekeeper, whose daughter had just been brutally whipped by her master:

> Thar's a day a comin'! Thar's a day a comin' . . . I hear de rumblin' ob de chariots! I see de flashin' ob de guns! White folks' blood is a-runnin' on de ground like a riber, an' de dead's heaped up dat high! . . . Oh, Lor'! hasten de day when de blows, an' de bruises, an' de aches, an' de pains, shall come to de white folks, an' de buzzards shall eat 'em as dey's dead in de streets. Oh, Lor'! roll on de chariots, an' gib de black people rest an' peace.[16]

Nor did slaves share the exaggerated optimism of white Americans about human ability. Trapped in a system from which there seemed little, if any, possibility of deliverance by human actions, they emphasized trusting in the Lord instead of trusting in man. Sermon after sermon and prayer after prayer echoed the words that Moses spoke on the banks of the Red Sea: "Stand still and see the salvation of the Lord." Though the leaders of the main three slave revolts, Gabriel in 1800, Denmark Vesey in 1822, and Nat Turner in 1831, all depended upon the Bible to justify and motivate rebellion, the major import of Exodus was to nurture internal resistance, not external revolution, among the slaves.

The story of Exodus contradicted the claim made by white Christians that God intended Africans to be slaves. Exodus proved that slavery was against God's will and that slavery inevitably would end, even though the when and the how remained hidden in the providence of God. Christian slaves thus applied the Exodus story, whose end they knew, to their own experience of slavery, which had not yet ended, and so gave meaning and purpose to lives threatened by senseless and demeaning brutality. Exodus functioned as an archetypal myth for the slaves. The sacred history of God's liberation of his people would be or was being reenacted in the American South. A white Union Army chaplain working among freedman in Decatur, Alabama, commented disapprovingly on the slaves' fascination with Exodus: "There is no part of the Bible with which they are so familiar as the story of the deliverance of Israel. Moses is their *ideal* of all that is high, and noble, and perfect, in man. I think they have been accustomed to regard Christ not so much in the light of a *spiritual* Deliverer, as that of a second Moses who would eventually lead *them* out of their prison-house of bondage."[19]

Thus, in the story of Israel's flight from Egypt, the slaves predicted a future radically different from their present. In times of despair, they remembered Exodus and found hope enough to endure the enormity of their suffering.

By appropriating the story of Exodus as their own story, black Christians articulated their own sense of peoplehood. Exodus symbolized their common history and common destiny. It would be hard to exaggerate the intensity of their identification with the children of Israel. AME pastor William Paul Quinn demonstrated how literal the metaphor of Exodus could become when he exhorted black Christians, "Let us comfort and encourage one another, and keep singing and shouting, great is the Holy One of Israel in the midst of us. Come thou Great Deliverer, once more awake thine almighty arm, and set thy African captives free."[20] As Quinn reveals, it was prayer and worship services that made the connection so immediate. Sermons, prayers, and songs recreated in the imagination of successive generations the travail and triumph of Israel.

Exodus became dramatically real, especially in the songs and prayer meetings of the slaves who reenacted the story as they shuffled in the ring dance they called the "Shout." In the ecstasy of worship, time and distance collapsed, and the slaves became the children of Israel. With the Hebrews, they traveled dry-shod through the Red Sea; they, too, saw Pharaoh's army "get drownded"; they stood beside Moses on Mount Pisgah and gazed out over the Promised Land; they crossed Jordan under Joshua and marched with him round the walls of Jericho. Their prayers for deliverance resonated with the experiential power of these liturgical dramas.

Identification with Israel, then, gave the slaves a communal identity as special, divinely favored people. This identity stood in stark contrast with racist propaganda depicting them as inferior to whites, destined by nature and providence to the status of slaves. The Exodus, the Promised Land, and Canaan were inextricably linked in their minds with the idea of freedom. Canaan referred not only to the condition of freedom but also to the territory of freedom, the North or Canada. As Frederick Douglass recalled, "A keen observer might have detected in our repeated singing of 'O Canaan, sweet Canaan, / I am bound for the land of Canaan,' something more than a hope of reaching heaven. We meant to reach the *North*, and the North was our Canaan."[21] Slave-owners, too, were well aware that the Exodus story could be a source of unflattering and perhaps subversive analogies. It took no genius to identify Pharaoh's army in the slave song "My army cross ober, My army cross ober, / O Pharaoh's army drownded."

The slaves' faith that God would free them just as he had Israel of old was validated by Emancipation. "Shout the glad tidings o'er Egypt's dark sea, / Jehovah has triumphed, his people are free!" the former slaves sang in celebration. But it did not take long for the freedmen to realize that Canaan Land still lay somewhere in the distance. "There must be no looking back to Egypt," a band of refugee slaves behind Union lines were instructed by a slave preacher in 1862. "Israel passed forty years in the wilderness, because of their unbelief. What if we cannot see right off the green fields of Canaan, Moses could not. He could not even see how to cross the Red Sea. If we would have greater freedom of body, we must free ourselves from the shackles of sin. . . . We must snap the chain of Satan, and educate ourselves and our children."[22] But as time went on and slavery was succeeded by other forms of racial oppression, black Americans seemed trapped in the wilderness no matter how hard they tried to escape. Former slave Charles Davenport voiced the despair of many when he recalled, "De preachers would exhort us dat us was de chillen o' Israel in de wilderness an' de Lord done sent us to take dis land o' milk and honey. But how us gwine-a take land what's already been took?"[23] When race relations reached a new low in the 1880s and 1890s, several black leaders turned to Africa as the Promised Land. Proponents of emigration, such as Alexander Crummell and Edward Wilmot Blyden, urged African-Americans to abandon the American wilderness for an African Zion. Few black Americans, however, heeded the call to emigrate to Africa; most continued to search for their Promised Land here. And as decade succeeded decade, they repeated the story that had for so many years kept their hopes alive. It was, then, a very old and evocative tradition that Martin Luther King echoed in his last sermon:

> We've got some difficult days ahead. But it really doesn't matter with me now. Because I've been to the mountaintop. Like anybody I would like to live a long life. Longevity has its place. But I'm not concerned about that now. I just want to do God's will. And He's allowed me to go up to the mountain. And I've *seen* the Promised Land. And I may not get there with you. But I want you to know tonight that we as a people will get to the Promised land.[24]

Between King's vision and Winthrop's vision of this American Promised Land, there stretches a period of more than three hundred years. The people who Winthrop addressed long ago took possession of their Promised Land. The people who King addressed still wait to enter theirs. For three centuries, white and black Americans have dwelled in the same land. For at least two of those centuries, they have shared the same religion. And yet during all those years, their national and religious identities have been radically opposed. It need not have been so. After all, Winthrop's version of Exodus and King's were not far apart. Both understood that charity is the charter that gives title to the Promised Land. Both taught that mercy, gentleness, and justice are the agreed upon terms for occupancy. Both remembered that the conditions of the contract had been set by God, not man. Occasionally, the two visions have come close to coinciding, as they did in the antislavery stance of the early Evangelicals, or in the abolitionist movement, or in Lincoln's profound realization that Americans were an "*almost* chosen people," or in the civil rights movement of our own era. Yet despite these moments of coherence, the meaning of Exodus for America remained fundamentally ambiguous. Was it Israel or was it Egypt?

Chapter Two

"Ethiopia Shall Soon Stretch Forth Her Hands": Black Destiny in Nineteenth-Century America

SUFFERING AND DESTINY

O N SUNDAY, JUNE 4, 1899, the Reverend Francis J. Grimke mounted his pulpit, looked out over his fashionable congregation, adjusted his spectacles, and began to preach the first of a three-part series of sermons. Grimke, a graduate of Princeton Theological Seminary (1878) and pastor of the Fifteenth Street Presbyterian Church in Washington, D.C., was no pulpit-pounding ex tempore preacher. His parishioners were used to the logical, intellectual, and somewhat dry style of his sermons. On this Sunday, especially, he wanted to calm, not arouse, emotion. Nevertheless, behind the measured phrases and calm tone, his feelings showed through. The text that morning was from Acts 7:57, the stoning of Stephen: "Then they cried with a loud voice, and stopped their ears, and ran upon him with one accord, and cast him out of the city, and stoned him." Grimke's topic was lynching.[1]

Between 1889 and 1899, 1,240 black men and women were lynched in the United States, mainly, but not exclusively, in the South. In 1898 alone, white mobs had seized and murdered 104 black people. The victims' names, when known, were tallied month by month by some black newspapers. Their alleged crimes, posted as well, ranged from murder, rape, and arson to

37

theft, "talking back," and "no charge." Accounts of the death of one victim in particular attracted Grimke's notice. Two months earlier, Sam Hose, a black man accused of assault and murder, had been burned alive by a white mob in Newnan, just outside Atlanta, Georgia. According to the newspapers, local whites celebrated the atrocity as a festive occasion. Close to 2,000 citizens, eager to get to the lynching on time, purchased tickets for the short train ride from Atlanta to Newnan. Along the route, women on porch steps waived handkerchiefs at the passing cars. Hundreds arrived too late to watch Hose die, but they pressed on anyway to see the charred corpse and to collect some souvenir of the day's outing. It was April 28, 1899—a Sunday.[2]

Grimke was shocked less by the lynching than he was by the spectators' enjoyment of it. How could people who claimed to be Christian go out and, on the very day of the Lord, do such things? How could the American church "with 135,667 preachers and more than 2,000,000 church members" permit "this awful, black record of murder and lawlessness?" How could it be that at this late date, a whole generation after slavery, blacks were still "a weak and defenseless race" at the mercy of a "Negro-hating nation?"[3] Race relations, on the eve of a new century, were worsening, not improving. Disfranchisement eroded the small gains blacks had won during Reconstruction; unprotected by the federal government, southern blacks had no recourse under a system of laws enforced by local whites.

Confronting the situation of his race in 1899, Grimke, like generations of black pastors before, had to find some meaning, some message of hope in all this misfortune, lest his people despair. "I know that things cannot go on as they are going on now," he told them. "I place my hope not on government, not on political parties, but on faith in the power of the religion of Jesus Christ to conquer all prejudices, to break down all walls of separation, and to weld together men of all races in one great brotherhood."[4]

Grimke's claim that the power of Christianity would solve the problem of racism was hopeful, but not naively optimistic. The facts of his own life did not support an easy or simplistic belief in Christian progress. Grimke had learned at an early age the perversity and intransigence of American prejudice. His mother was a slave; his father was his master. After his father died, Grimke's white half-brother attempted to enslave him despite the provisions of their father's will. At the age of ten, Francis Grimke became a runaway slave. Captured several years later, he almost died in a Charleston workhouse where his brother had him jailed as a fugitive. After release, he was sold to a Confederate army officer, whom he served for the duration of the war. Grimke did not find it easy to regard whites as brothers. Even in the church, within his own denomination, he had experienced the spirit of caste in acts of overt discrimination. If Christianity were to triumph, it would be in spite of the American church, which he castigated in print as "an apostate church, utterly unworthy of the name which it bears."[5]

Yet Grimke did not despair. He kept faith in the power of Christianity to change the world, and this belief was validated by other events in his life. After the war, he had been educated and assisted North through the generosity of whites. At Lincoln University and Princeton Seminary, he had been instructed and respected by white professors. Most surprising of all, he had met and formed close family ties with two of his father's sisters, his white aunts, Sarah and Angelina Grimke, of antislavery fame.[6] From Charleston jail to Princeton Seminary, from betrayed brother to beloved nephew, from slave to prominent cleric: the trajectory of Grimke's own life contradicted despair. He was hopeful, then, that the racial situation would, in time, improve, but his hope strained in tension with his alienation from the nation and the church. Hope and alienation echoed through his sermons like some dissonant chord:

In spite of the shallowness and emptiness and glaring hypocrisy
. . . of the church . . . I still believe that Christianity is in this land.
Today it is like a little grain of mustard seed, but it has entered the
soil, has germinated, and is springing up. It is like the little lump
of leaven which the woman hid in three measures of meal: but it
has begun to work, and will go on working, diffusing itself, until
the whole is leavened. God has promised to give to his Son the hea-
then for his inheritance, and the uttermost parts of the earth for his
possession: and in that promise this land is included. Christianity
shall one day have sway even in Negro-hating America; the spirit
which it inculcates . . . is sure, sooner or later, to prevail. I have,
myself, here and there, seen its mighty transforming power. I have
seen white men and women under its regenerating influence lose
entirely the caste feeling. . . . Jesus Christ is yet to reign in this
land. I will not see it, you will not see it, but it is coming all the
same. In the growth of Christianity, true, real, genuine Christianity
in this land, I see the promise of better things for us as a race.[7]

In 1899, most white Americans, and some blacks as well,
would have rejected Grimke's sermon as bitter and intemperate.
He had libeled the nation whose destiny it was to Christianize and
democratize the world, an "obligation" already undertaken in the
Philippines. Some blacks, like the majority of whites, would have
regarded the ideal of racial harmony envisaged in his sermon as a
misguided and impractical dream. Blacks had no future in this
white man's country and should emigrate back to Africa. A few,
very few, blacks would have criticized his slavish allegiance to
Christianity. The true religious identity of the black race was
either Islam or Judaism. For that matter, there were those, as there
always had been, who found any religion, meaningless in the
struggle for freedom. But in 1899 the majority of black Americans
would have agreed with Grimke that the ultimate solution to the
"Negro problem" was to be found in Christianity, a Christianity,
to be sure, unlike that of white Americans. With Grimke, they

would have believed that blacks someday would take their rightful places in America, but an America transformed from the one they knew. They believed that the solution lay off in the future and were uncertain about the date and method of its achievement. They also believed that the present and the future were shaped by God's providence, in which they were assigned a particular role. In short, they believed that they had a destiny, and in that destiny the suffering of blacks like Sam Hose, and all those who preceded him, had meaning. These beliefs formed a theological tradition developed over the century, and in reaffirming that tradition, Grimke and his congregation reaffirmed the meaning of their lives.

That blacks had a divinely appointed destiny, no black Christian in the nineteenth century denied. But what was it? Since its fulfillment was still to come, who could be certain of its features? By what right did anyone identify this or that event as God's plan for the race? Black spokesmen, mainly clerical but also lay, struggled with this quandary in sermons, speeches, tracts, convention minutes, history books, resolutions, and editorials, from the beginning of the nineteenth century to the end. They searched the Bible, God's word, for signs of his will for the race. To interpret historical events, they looked to the bible for precedents (or paradigms) and for prophecies (or predictions). They found both in two texts that served as the classical loci for interpreting black history in the nineteenth century: the book of Exodus and Psalms 68:31.

As long as slavery preoccupied the attention of antebellum blacks, the archetypal myth of Exodus dominated their thinking about black destiny. When slavery ended, as it did in the North early in the century, and oppression continued, even worsened, as it did in the 1830s and 1850s, black Americans read their future in Psalms 68:31: "Princes shall come out of Egypt and Ethiopia shall soon stretch forth her hands unto God." I do not mean to suggest that these texts were contradictory. In black religious thought and ritual, they were complementary. The intensity of slaves' identification with Israel had blunted the sharp edge of the question of why God had permitted slavery: We are Israel; God frees Israel.[8] But the underlying question remained. It was, of course, a particular instance of the universal problem of evil: why does God permit the innocent to suffer? At certain times during the nineteenth century, the more basic question pushed to the fore of black thought with great urgency. As J. Sella Martin lamented in the August 26, 1865, issue of the *Christian Recorder*: "Has Providence so little care for human lives as to permit the sacrifice of over a million of them for the purpose of overthrowing the system of slavery, only that its victims may be treated worse than slaves after they are free?" Martin was disturbed by the denial of suffrage for the freedman (indeed, for black men in general). The pressure of events ineluctably moved black religious thought beyond Exodus toward Job. In response, black clergy and laity meditated upon Psalms 68:31 as well as on Exodus. In addition to linking the present with the mythic past, they joined it to a mythic future when "princes shall come out of Egypt and Ethiopia shall soon stretch forth her hands unto God," without doubt the most quoted verse in black religious history.

In the destiny of the black race, predicted in Psalms 68:31, African-American Christians thought they could read the meaning of black suffering. But they confronted an immediate problem: unlike the book of Exodus, whose narrative was clear and easy to interpret, the verse in Psalms was obscure. Yet its very obscurity extended its explanatory range. Consequently, nineteenth-century interpretations of Psalms 68:31 differed widely. They all, however, clustered around three major themes: "the African race," "the redemption of Africa," and "the mission of the darker races."

THE AFRICAN RACE

All interpreters of the verse agreed that Egypt and Ethiopia referred to "the African race." In a kind of mythic geography,

nineteenth-century black Americans identified Ethiopia and
Egypt with their own African origins and looked to those ancient
civilizations as exemplars of a glorious African past, surely as legitimate a fictive pedigree as white American claims of descent
from Greco-Roman civilization. "Ancient history, as well as holy
writ, informs us of the national greatness of our progenitors,"
boasted African Methodist minister William Miller, in a sermon
delivered in 1810. A host of black preachers and historians
throughout the century substantially agreed with his sketch of the
black past: "The inhabitants of Africa are descended from the ancient inhabitants of Egypt, a people once famous for science of
every description." Biblical, archaeological, and historical evidence was marshaled by black scholars to prove that descendants
of Egypt and Ethiopia had nothing to fear from any invidious
comparison with the descendants of Europe. The vaunted superiority of Anglo-Saxon civilization was merely the empty boast of
ignorant men. According to black historians, the "Children of
Ham were clearly the first to lead off in the march of civilization."
From the Egyptians, the torch had passed to the Greeks, from
them to the Romans, and from the Romans, finally, and belatedly,
to the Europeans. While the Egyptians were establishing law and
political institutions, the sons of Japhet, the Europeans, were still
"a savage race of men," "inhabiting the rocks and caverns, a
wretched prey to wild beast and to one another." Hosea Easton, a
minister from Hartford, could not resist digging in the point: "I
would here remark that it is a little singular that modern philosophers, the descendants of this race of savages, should claim for
their race a superiority of intellect over those who, at that very
time, were enjoying all the real benefits of civilized life."⁹

Nineteenth-century blacks needed to reclaim for themselves a
civilized African past in order to refute the charge that they were
inherently inferior, especially because they, by and large, assumed
that modern Africans and African-Americans were less civilized
than Anglo-Americans. Most would have reluctantly concurred

with William Wells Brown, escaped slave, novelist, lecturer, and historian, who in 1863 wrote: "I admit that the condition of my race . . . at the present time cannot compare favorably with the Anglo-Saxon." The disability of the race, however, was due to the circumstances of enslavement and oppression forced upon it by whites. The historical evidence indicated that once the reverse had been the case. But Egypt and Ethiopia had fallen. What had happened? Grown prosperous, they had, according to William Miller, forgotten God and turned aside to idolatry. "Where nations have turned aside to idolatry they have lost their civilization," explained black historian George Washington Williams. Hosea Easton placed the blame upon war. Whatever the cause, the fall from former glory had been great. African-Americans, lamented Easton, are "the remnant of a once noble but now heathenish people," as different from their ancestors as they are from other races. Williams theorized that "the genuine African has gradually degenerated into the typical Negro," "the lowest strata" of the once great African race. According to Miller, God's wrath was so aroused by the idolatry of Africans and Ethiopians that he pronounced judgment upon them through his prophet Isaiah: "Like as my servant Isaiah hath walked naked and barefooted three years, for a sign and wonder upon Egypt and Ethiopia, so shall the king of Assyria lead the Egyptian prisoners and Ethiopian captives, young and old, naked and barefooted, even with their bodies uncovered; to the shame of Egypt" (Isaiah 20:3–4). "My brethren," exclaimed Miller to his free black congregation, "you have all seen this prophecy astonishingly fulfilled even to a very late period, upon the unhappy Africans." Miller seems to have been unique in seeing the slave trade as the literal enactment of Isaiah's prophecy, but all black interpreters linked the decline of African civilization with moral degradation.[10]

Yet if princes had once ruled wisely in Egypt and if Ethiopia had seen the birth of civilization, might not their descendants in

America, now Christianized and civilized, restore their rightful dignity among the nations? Could this have been the meaning of slavery: the education, elevation, and regeneration of the descendants of idolatrous Egypt and fallen Ethiopia? A number of articulate black clergymen thought so.

THE REDEMPTION OF AFRICA

As early as 1808, in one of the earliest black sermons extant, Absalom Jones, pastor of St. Thomas's African Episcopal Church in Philadelphia, offered this answer to the question, Why has God permitted slavery? "It has always been a mystery," he confessed, "why the impartial Father of the human race should have permitted the transportation of so many millions of our fellow creatures to this country, to endure all the miseries of slavery. . . . Perhaps his design was, that a knowledge of the gospel might be acquired by some of their descendants, in order that they might become qualified to be the messengers of it, to the land of their fathers." The reticence of "Perhaps his design was" no doubt was due in part to Jones's reluctance to presume that he or any man knew for certain God's will, but it also sprang from another troubling fact. As Jones and other black ministers well knew, the evangelization and civilization of blacks was the rationale used by Europeans, from the mid fifteenth century on, to justify enslaving Africans. In other words, this explanation came dangerously close to absolving whites of their guilt for slavery. The black clergy refused absolution by distinguishing God's will from his permission. God wills good; he only permits evil, and from it draws good. Although "God permitted these things to come to pass," William Miller preached, "it does not follow that the oppressors of Africa are less culpable for their savage treatment to the unoffending Africans." George Washington Williams echoed the sentiment two generations later: "God often permits evil on the ground of man's free agency but he does not commit evil. The Negro of this country can turn to his Saxon brothers and say, as Joseph said to his brethren who wickedly sold him, 'As for you, ye meant it unto evil, but God meant it unto good; that we, after learning your arts and sciences, might return to Egypt and deliver the rest of our brethren who are yet in the house of bondage.' "[11]

Few questioned why it was necessary for Africans to learn these arts and sciences at the price of so much suffering. God chastises those he chooses. Through suffering, God was purifying Ethiopia's sons in America in order to make them "a chosen generation, a royal priesthood, and an holy nation, a peculiar people." The will of God is hidden in mystery, as Job long ago learned: "Be still and know that I am God! Clouds and darkness are round about me; yet righteousness and judgement are the habitation of my throne. I do my will and pleasure in the heavens above, and in the earth beneath; it is my sovereign prerogative to bring good out of evil and cause the wrath of man to praise me, and the remainder of that wrath I will restrain."[12] These were not so much answers as they were genuflections before the mystery of divine providence. The benevolence of that providence was assured by events: the abolition of the African slave trade on January 1, 1808, the abolition of slavery in New York on July 4, 1827, the emancipation of the British West Indies in 1834, and finally emancipation in the United States in 1865. These were indices of "the goodness of God, and his wisdom in all things." They were divine pledges that the psalmist's prediction was being fulfilled in the elevation, education, and progress of the African race in America.[13]

The purpose of God, revealing itself in human history, was the redemption of the African race. Slavery was his means for achieving this end—good drawn out of evil. But this was not all that Psalms 68:31 meant. The redemption of the African race included the redemption of Africa itself. The sons of Ethiopia, now enlightened by the Christian gospel, would return to Africa and rekindle the flame of religion and civilization snuffed out by idolatry so long ago. This, too, was God's will. However, nineteenth-century black preachers who espoused this view, as did most, faced a problem, the American Colonization Society. Founded in 1816 as a benevolent reform society, the ACS proposed a solution to the problem of slavery: the emancipation and repatriation of slaves in Africa. While the black clergy favored the evangelization of Africa and the emigration of those blacks who wished to return to Africa, they feared and condemned the ACS for plotting to forcibly remove free blacks from the United States in order to squelch antislavery agitation. Instead of gradually eroding slavery, the ACS, in their view, was bent on preserving and strengthening it. In response to this threat, black leaders spoke out against colonization in pulpit, platform, and press. Increasingly, the self-referents of blacks changed from "African" and "sons of Ethiopia," to "free colored" and "American." Increasingly, black spokesmen elaborated on the contributions of blacks to America, their participation in her wars, their blood and sweat shed on her soil. "African-Americans are here to stay" was a leitmotif through most of the conventions, editorials, and resolutions of the nineteenth century, both before the Civil War and after.[14]

To be sure, there were blacks who encouraged emigration, always voluntary, and who actually chose to emigrate themselves. Paul Cuffe in the late eighteenth century and Daniel Coker in 1820 had led expeditions to Sierra Leone. Moreover, during especially bad times, such as the 1830s, the 1850s, and the 1870s, emigration seemed more and more attractive as the only escape from white oppression. Martin Delany, before the war, and Henry McNeal Turner, after, argued strenuously for the benefits of emigration. Only in Africa, Turner maintained, could blacks fully assert their manhood rights, which, as far as he could see, this Negro-hating country would never recognize.[15]

Emigration, then, would fulfill two purposes: the Christianization of Africans and the colonization of Africa by African-Americans. Daniel Coker articulated the mixed, and to our eyes, ambiguous, motives of the emigrationists in a letter he mailed back to Maryland in 1820. "Oh, what a work is this," he exclaims. "What darkness has covered the minds of the people." Anyone "who loves souls would weep over them, and be willing to suffer and die with them." In a striking phrase, he confesses, "my soul cleaves to Africa. . . . I expect to give my life to bleeding, groaning, dark, benighted Africa." Then, without skipping a beat, Coker shifts from missionary zeal to mercantile calculation: "If you ask my opinion as to coming out;—I say, let all that can, sell out and come, come and bring ventures, to trade, etc., and you may do much better than you can possibly do in America, and not work half so hard. . . . Bring . . . two hogsheads of good leaf tobacco, cheap calico, and cheap handkerchiefs, pins, knives and forks, pocket knives, etc., with these you may buy land, hire hands, or buy provisions. I say, come—the land is good."[16]

Nineteenth-century black Americans presumed, as we have seen, that Africa needed their help. The African, according to an article published in the *AME Church Review* in 1890, "has made few strides along the line of intelligence; his sight has long become dimmed to apprehend his Maker. He has declined in the scale of human intelligence. He gropes in darkness. He has wandered from the shining face of his God into gross ignorance. The twentieth century of his Redeemer's advent dawns upon him sunk in superstition, and worshipping the creature more than the Creator."[17]

Alexander Crummell the chief American advocate in the later nineteenth century for the evangelization of Africa and himself a missionary to Liberia for twenty years, reminded African-Americans of their duty to assist the simple, childlike Africans to the higher level of civilization that blacks in America already possessed. Though Crummell praised the natural modesty and generosity of the native Africans as superior to the immorality and corruption of the English and Americans, it was clear that the African stood in sore need of the blessings of technological civilization. In this regard, Crummell and other proponents of African missions revealed a deep ambivalence about Africa. On the one hand, they presumed that Africans were backward pagans. On the other, they knew from bitter experience that white Americans were racist, imperialistic, and materialistic. Europeans were superior in civilization, Africans in natural religiosity.[18]

Without Christianity, however, the African's inclination toward religion remained unfulfilled, perverted by idolatry, or misguided into Islam. It was the proper mission of the African-American to bring the African to the gospel. Whites had no business in Africa. As Emmanuel K. Love observed before the Black Baptist Foreign Mission Convention in 1889, "There is no doubt in my mind that Africa is our field of operation and that [as] Moses was sent to deliver his brethren, and as the prophets were members of the race to whom they were sent, so I am convinced that God's purpose is to redeem Africa through us." "This work," he concluded, "is ours by appointment, by inheritance, and by choice." Europeans had failed to Christianize the "dark continent" despite previous attempts. African-Americans would succeed, according to J. Sella Martin, because they could withstand the hostile climate that decimated whites and, more important, because their skin color would arouse the confidence, not the distrust, of the natives. Edward Wilmot Blyden argued that history itself proved that God intended Africa for black missionaries. By allowing slavery, God converted them; by permitting racism, he directed them back; and by completely shutting up the vast interior of Africa from exploration, "until the time arrived for the emancipation of her children in the Western World," God had clearly singled out black people as his chosen instrument to redeem Africa.[19]

A few dissenting voices denied that the redemption of Africa was the divinely appointed destiny of black Americans. For example, T. Thomas Fortune, militant editor of the *New York Age*, complained: "The talk about the black people being brought to this country to prepare themselves to evangelize Africa is so much religious nonsense boiled down to a sycophantic platitude. The Lord who is eminently just, had no hand in their forcibly coming here, it was preeminently the work of the devil. Africa will have to be evangelized from *within*, not *from without*."[20] Fortune had economics but not symbolism on his side of the argument. Black churches, in fact, were too poor to mount a large-scale African campaign, and attempts to work through the missionary boards of white denominations ran into racial difficulties. Nevertheless, the idea of African missions loomed large in the consciousness of black Christians from 1870 on. Their experience of oppression seemed to verify the contours of Turner and Blyden's racial map: Africa stood for opportunity and manhood, America for discrimination and emasculation. Few African-Americans actually ventured the trip, but symbolically the mission to redeem Africa confirmed their importance as a people. Reflecting this attitude, the logo of the influential AME journal, the *Christian Recorder*, was redesigned. After 1869, the plain title in bold type gave way to a picture of the globe, turned to the continent of Africa. Three sailing ships from America draw near the western coast of Africa. Rays of light shoot out from the "dark continent," and beneath the globe stretches the banner, "Ethiopia shall soon stretch forth her hands to God."

As they imagined the future of redeemed Africa, nineteenth-century black writers reversed old stereotypes about the dark continent. George Washington Williams, for example, depicted this idyllic scene: "The sabbath bells will summon from scattered cottages smiling populations, linked together by friendship, and happy in all the sweetness of domesticated charities. Thus the glory of her latter day shall be greater than at the beginning, and *Ethiopia shall stretch forth her hands unto God*." Edward Blyden, in 1862, foresaw a less pastoral and more active future: "Africa will furnish a development of civilization which the world has never yet witnessed. Its great peculiarity will be its moral development." A generation earlier, Hosea Easton had placed Africa "in the front ranks of the church, when she marches into the millennial era." The progression from the fall of Africa, to the redemption of Africa, to the future of Africa particularized the salvation of mankind in the history of the "African race." Viewing history from the perspective of Psalms 68:31, black theologians in the nineteenth century had divined a salvation-history for their people. They did not stop there; a few took a step beyond.[21]

THE MISSION OF THE DARKER RACES

Consistently, black Americans condemned American Christianity as hypocritical and false. Slavery and race hatred blatantly violated the Christian law of love. The indictment of John Edward Bruce, a newspaper columnist, written in 1891, may serve as a summary of most of the charges elaborated over the century:

> [The] white church of America . . . preaches and perverts the Gospel, . . . by indirection and evasion denies the fatherhood of God and the brotherhood of man, . . . makes the Black man who loves Jesus feel his inferiority and that he is a degree or two lower than the white Christian and a *ward* rather than an equal before God. . . . Judgement is coming! The noisome pestilence that walketh in darkness will have no terrors for the Godly, but they will as surely overtake the great majority of the Negro-hating white Christians as that God is just. And He is just, for He intended that his holy religion should enfold in its broad mantle, in the perfect equality of Democracy, every human being on earth, for He is no respecter of persons. The white American Christian is. Therefore, his religion is a religion of lies and hypocrisy. Is this plain enough?[22]

Two points in Bruce's brief against white Christians merit elaboration: first, his prediction of divine retribution, and second, his implicit critique of civil religion.

A great deal of the criticism leveled against American Christianity by African-Americans took the form of an apocalyptic warning, articulated best by David Walker in 1830. "Unless, America repents and soon, God will tear up the very face of the earth!"[23] In Walker's *Appeal to the Coloured Citizens*, and in other black jeremiads as well, God appears as the Lord of History, the Ruler of Nations, who reveals his will in events of the day. In effect, the jeremiad did more than enable blacks to vent their righteous indignation; it placed black Christians in a stance of judgment over white Christians; it consolidated a position of moral superiority for the descendants of the African race. As we shall see shortly, black theologians, in the late nineteenth century, extended the doctrine of black moral superiority from a national to a global scale.

Nineteenth-century blacks accused the nation of betraying not only Christianity but democracy, the national faith recorded in the national scriptures (the Declaration of Independence and the Constitution) and celebrated on the national holy day (July 4th). Deep alienation from the religion of the republic prompted the First Annual Convention of the People of Colour to pass a resolution in 1831 urging blacks "throughout the United States" to "set apart the fourth day of July, as a day of humiliation, fasting and prayer—and to beseech Almighty God to interpose on our behalf, that the shackles of slavery may be broken, and our sacred rights obtained." In 1865, the Washington, D.C., correspondent of the *Christian Recorder* reported that the Fourth of July celebration at Union Bethel AME Church "was the first Fourth of July of the colored people."[24]

Thus African-Americans scorned the Christianity of whites and questioned the civil religion of the nation. Some were driven away from Christianity by the race prejudice of white Christians, but most did not reject the gospel or the principles of democracy. In their critiques of American Christianity, blacks implicitly and sometimes explicitly cast themselves as the models of true Christianity in America. As Levi Coppin, editor of the *AME Church Review*, remarked in 1890, African-Americans thought that "this question of civilization [was] by no means settled": "We are firmly of the opinion that the best expression of Christian civilization is yet to be seen, and who knows but that some of the very characteristics of the Negro that are discounted by the present civilization, are the very things needed for that higher and better which is yet to come." The characteristics of the Negro that Coppin had in mind had by this time become standard in black sermons: the list included patience, humility, meekness, peacefulness, long suffering, kindness, charitableness—in a word, Christ-likeness. Notice that these virtues characterized not just individuals but the race as a whole. The "natural religious temperament" of the African race had been molded by providence into the imitation of Christ. These were the virtues that had to replace the jingoism, imperialism, racism, and materialism of America if Christian civilization were to become a reality. Coppin only hinted at what others boldly stated. "It is my solemn belief, that if ever the world becomes Christianized . . . it will be through the means, under God of the *Blacks*, who are now held in wretchedness, and degradation, by the white *Christians* of the world," claimed David Walker. The fourth national Negro convention in 1834 purposely alluded to the early Christians when it proclaimed that "our very sighs and groans like the blood of martyrs will prove to have been the seed of the church." One overzealous AME minister narrowed the mission of the race to the clergy of his own denomination, who were "the instruments in the hands of God for the redemption of Africa, the subjugation of America, and for bringing the world unto God and his Christ." In a less grandiose and more poetic style, the American Moral Reform Society of 1837 spoke of black faces "as so many Bibles, that shall warn this guilty nation of her injustice."[25]

The mission of black Christians to be the leaven of true Christian civilization was elaborated in greatest detail by two black theologians of the late nineteenth century. Theophilus Gould Steward and James Theodore Holly moved the interpretation of Psalms 68:31 to a new global perspective. Both men insisted that the psalmist had predicted a special role for the darker races in the millennial phase of history, the end time. Steward, a minister of the AME Church, concluded in 1888 that the evidence of Scripture and the signs of the times indicated the end of the present age was near. Western Christianity had nothing more to offer believers; it could no longer speak to them with authority. Indeed, an end to the militaristic and racist corruption of Christianity by the West had to come if the pagan nations were ever to have the true gospel preached to them. Fratricidal warfare among the "Christian nations" would end the present age and a new and final age of a raceless and peaceful Christianity would begin, in which the darker, non-Christian peoples of the world (Africans, Indians, Chinese) would hear and accept the pure gospel of Christ, undefiled by Anglo-Saxon prejudice. This new religious age, Steward speculated, might well be led by the Church of Abyssinia, a "hidden church in the wilderness," which "God has maintained for himself as a witness," down through the centuries. "Then the really righteous unobscured by the perverse civilization—a civilization which is called Christian, but which is essentially Saxon—shall shine forth as the sun, and this hidden church of the wilderness shall come forth to lead Africa's millions, as a part of that fullness of the Gentiles which is to come to welcome the universal Christ."[26]

James Theodore Holly also defined a universal role in the end time for the darker races. According to Holly, writing in 1884, the "divine plan of human redemption" unfolds in three historic periods or dispensations. The first dispensation belonged to the Semitic race, whose task it was to formulate, write down, and preserve the Holy Scriptures. The second, or Japhetic, phase coincided with the apostolic or evangelical period, the age of the Europeans, who had been commissioned to spread the gospel. The Hebrew dispensation ended with the destruction of the Temple in A.D. 70. The Japhetic phase would end in warfare, after which the millennium would commence. During this thousand-year reign of peace and justice, the Hamitic race would bring to completion the divine plan of human redemption only imperfectly realized by the Semitic and Japhetic races. To the sons of Ham, "the elect among nations," "the crowning work of the will of God is reserved for the millennial phase of Christianity when Ethiopia shall stretch out her hands directly unto God." The Semites preserved the word of God, the Japhites preached it; during this last and greatest dispensation, the Hamites would put the word of God into practice. In a striking reversal of the legend of Noah's curse of Canaan, Holly explained why:

> The African race has been the servant of servants to their brethren of the other races during all the long and dreary ages of the Hebrew and Christian dispensations. And it is this service that they have so patiently rendered through blood and tears that shall finally obtain for them the noblest places of service in the Coming Kingdom. That what has been a curse to them under Gentile tyranny will become a blessing to them under the mild and beneficent reign of Christ, and thus will be realized the double but adverse significations of the Hebrew word *barak* . . . which signifies to "bless," and also "to curse." . . . The curse of Canaan, dooming him to be a servant of servants unto his brethren, which lowered him to a place of dishonor under the earthly governments of men, will turn to a blessing unto him and exalt him to the posts of honor under the heavenly government of God.[27]

Steward and Holly pushed the interpretation of Psalms 68:31 as far as it could go in explaining human history—all the way to the millennium. In the process, they shifted the understanding of black destiny from a particularistic to a universal role. Reflecting upon their experience of suffering as a people, black Americans in the nineteenth century fashioned a theology of history whose conclusions, clumsily summarized, were these: Those who oppress and enslave others, those who make war, those who spread "civilization" by conquest, those who degrade other races, those who corrupt Christianity by making it a clan religion, are destined to destroy one another. Their age will shortly end. A new age will soon begin. In this new age, it will be the destiny of those who were oppressed but did not oppress, those who were enslaved but did not enslave, those who were hated but did not hate, to realize the gospel on earth.

Both Holly and Steward expected the age of Japheth to end soon. A twentieth-century skeptic might point out that it did not end soon enough to save Sam Hose, much less Mack Parker or Emmett Till. The skeptic would, of course, be right, but also would have missed the point. "Princes shall come out of Egypt and Ethiopia shall soon stretch forth her hands unto God" was not so much a prophecy as it was a prayer.

Chapter Three

"How Far the Promised Land?"
Black Religion and Black Protest

O N DECEMBER 1, 1955, a black seamstress named Rosa Parks boarded a bus in Montgomery, Alabama. Buses in Montgomery, the "Cradle of the Confederacy," had always been segregated. Blacks sat in back; whites sat up front. If the bus was full, blacks were required to give up their seats to whites and ride standing in the aisle. Bus drivers insulted black passengers and even made them get off the bus and reenter by the back door, after they had paid their fares. The bus system of Montgomery, like others throughout the South, stood as a daily reminder of the pervasiveness of Jim Crow.

Mrs. Parks found a seat in the front of the section reserved for "Colored" and sat down. As the bus grew crowded with people heading home from work, no seats were available for new passengers boarding the bus. The driver ordered Mrs. Parks and three black passengers next to her to get up and give their seats to whites. The others complied. Rosa Parks stayed seated, until a policeman came and placed her under arrest.

Later accounts would explain that she refused to move simply because she was tired. But the story was more complex. Mrs. Parks had worked for the secretary for the local branch of the NAACP. The Montgomery NAACP had been trying for several months to develop a test case to challenge state segregation laws.

As a matter of fact, one and a half years before the arrest, the Women's Political Council, a group of politically active black Montgomery women, had written to the mayor demanding improved treatment of black bus riders and threatening a bus boycott if their plea went unheeded. Mrs. Parks's arrest was perfectly timed. News of the arrest spread quickly in the black community. That evening, several black women, some of them active in the Women's Political Council, headed by Mrs. Jo Ann Robinson, professor of English at Alabama State College, concluded that blacks should retaliate by boycotting the buses. They broached the idea with E. D. Nixon, director of the NAACP chapter in Montgomery, and he began phoning black ministers and other community leaders to mobilize a boycott. For almost a year, blacks in Montgomery stayed off the buses. Despite court injunctions and police harassment, despite threats and bombings, despite the arrest, trial, and conviction of their leaders, they stayed off the buses. And on November 13, 1956, they won: the United States Supreme Court upheld a lower court decision declaring Alabama laws requiring segregation on buses unconstitutional.

Though it was preceded by a successful boycott of segregated buses in Baton Rouge, Louisiana, the more famous Montgomery bus boycott initiated a new era in the struggle of American blacks for racial justice. As the first widely noted mass protest mounted by black people in the Deep South, it signaled and inspired a new militancy among African-Americans. Montgomery attracted the attention of the nation and dramatized for more Americans than ever before the reality of segregation. During the boycott, tactics evolved that would be used again and again in the civil rights protests of the 1960s. Moreover, Montgomery catapulted to fame the twenty-six-year-old pastor of Dexter Avenue Baptist Church, Martin Luther King, Jr. He, better than any other leader, would articulate the religious meaning of civil rights for the nation.

Montgomery, then, was a watershed. It marked something new

in the history of race relations in this country. Yet it also represented something old—the perennial exhortation to the nation to "rise up and live out the meaning of its creed," as King declared at the 1963 March on Washington. Montgomery, and in large part, the civil rights movement that ensued, was a revival, an attempt to reawaken the nation to ideals upon which it was founded. This revival, like those of the past, echoed the old biblical themes. Once again, the God who had acted in Israel's history was acting in America's. "God had decided to use Montgomery as the proving ground for the struggle and triumph of freedom and justice in America," remarked King in his written account of the bus boycott.[1]

The tendency to cast political and social events as scenes in the drama of salvation was a familiar habit to Americans, accustomed to envisioning the United States as God's New Israel and themselves as a chosen people. Over the years, clusters of images had formed into a complex and powerful myth. Some of these images were scriptural in origin; others derived from the rhetoric of the Revolution and the republican tradition of the Constitution. Whatever their source, these images conveyed the durable belief that America was special. Of all the nations, America had been singled out to save (or help save) the world. Within this myth of exceptionalism, Americans from diverse lands, diverse faiths, and diverse peoples embraced a common identity, invented a common history, and projected a common destiny. King, and those he spoke for, invoked the national myth. But at the same time, he reaffirmed another set of beliefs that rose out of the profound ambivalence that African-Americans felt toward the selfsame myth. Denied at first freedom and then equality in America, blacks had protested by decrying slavery and discrimination as fundamental violations of American ideals. To the extent that they criticized white Americans for failing to live the national creed, they tended to assume the myth of exceptionalism. But as racism proved intransigent and as blacks continued to be defined as aliens in their own land, they began to perceive the myth itself as wrong.

Public black protest began early in the nation's history. As soon as British colonists in North America began to claim that their rights had been violated by England, enslaved Africans took occasion to claim their right to liberty upon the same grounds. In 1774, blacks in Massachusetts petitioned the governor and the general court to grant them freedom, arguing that

> we have in common with all other men a naturel right to our freedoms without Being deprived of them by our fellow men as we are a freeborn Pepel and have never forfeited this Blessing by aney compact or agreement whatever. But we were unjustly dragged by the cruel hand of power from our dearest frinds and sum of us stolen from the bosoms of our tender Parents . . . and Brought hither to be made slaves for Life in a Christian land.[2]

Slavery, they went on to argue, violated not only natural law but also the fundamental commandment of Christianity: "There is a grat number of us sencear members of the Church of Christ. How can the master be said to Beare my Borden when he Beares me down with the Have chanes of slavery and [oppression] against my will." This and several more petitions like it were ignored. Although Revolution and its aftermath would bring freedom to some slaves, for the vast majority, slavery "within a free and Christian nation" would still be the lot of their children's children.

During the late eighteenth century, another revolution held out a promise of freedom to black Americans. The spread of Evangelical Christianity, with its emphasis on the necessity of conversion, tended to level everyone in the eyes of God and, for a while at least, in the eyes of men as well. Social status and racial hierarchy were undercut by the biracial religious communities formed in the Methodist class meetings and the Baptist conventicles. In these gatherings, the poor, the uneducated, and the enslaved were permitted to pray, exhort, and even preach. In the emotional tumult of the revivals, racial barriers were momentarily transcended as whites converted blacks and blacks converted whites. When the Methodists and some Baptists condemned slavery as a moral evil, it seemed that white and black Christians were about to preach the same gospel of freedom.

But the Evangelical revolution, no less than the political revolution, proved in the end to be incomplete. By the turn of the century, Methodists and Baptists had retreated from earlier anti-slavery positions in the face of stiff opposition from southern Christians. Moreover, the increase in African Methodists and Baptists was disquieting to whites, who began to feel uneasy about worshiping in the company of so many blacks. Seating them in galleries and back pews kept them out of sight, if not out of mind. Even separate black congregations suffered discriminatory treatment from white clergy anxious to keep control over the "brethren in black." Convinced that biracial fellowship really meant white control, black Christians by the 1820s had successfully established their own independent churches.

All evidence to the contrary, African-Americans insisted that American liberty and Christian brotherhood were meant to include them. Most refused to believe that America was a white man's country or that Christianity was a white man's religion. When white Christians discriminated against them in church or preached that slavery and Christianity were compatible, they built their own churches, if possible, and preached that Christianity and slavery were antithetical. Christianity was not false; the American version of it was. When whites, in the antebellum period, spoke of America as a Christian nation and predicted that the millennium would begin on these shores, blacks protested that any Christianity that compromised with slavery corrupted the religion of Jesus. Implicit in this criticism of "slaveholding religion" was the assumption that black Americans were the true disciples of Jesus in the nation. The act of calling America to account for betraying her covenant with the Lord placed the black critics, as they well knew, in the long line of biblical prophets, apostles, and martyrs, who, each in their own time, dared to speak truth to power. Moreover, it was the paradox of the Christian gospel that salvation came through the oppressed and the suffering, rather than the high and the mighty. Had not the Redeemer himself come as a "suffering servant"? This being so, who in America resembled him more, the master or the slave?

The redemptive mission of blacks clashed with the dominant myth of America. Nothing displays this cultural dissonance more clearly than the image of an American Israel. As the spirituals eloquently attest, slaves appropriated the story of Exodus to account for their own experience as a people. Free blacks expounded on the analogy between Egypt and white America and explicated the similarities between Israel and black America in scores of addresses, sermons, and pamphlets. God, they insisted, would act again, as he had of old, to save his people; their oppressors, he would destroy. In the words of David Walkers's widely circulated jeremiad: "God rules in the armies of heaven and among the inhabitants of the earth, having his ears continually open to the tears and groans of his oppressed people, and being . . . just and holy . . . will . . . one day appear fully in behalf of the oppressed, and arrest the progress of the avaricious." And in terms that proved strikingly prophetic, Walker warned Americans that God overthrew oppressors by causing "them to rise up one against another, to be split and divided . . . to oppress each other, and . . . to open hostilities with sword in hand."[3]

The Civil War and Emancipation seemed to validate African-American identification with Israel, but blacks discovered that racial oppression showed no signs of abating. Decades after Emancipation, they still had not entered the Promised Land. Against the background of disfranchisement, lynching, and newly established codes of segregation in the late nineteenth century, blacks struggled to understand what their destiny in America might mean. As we've seen, one interpretation explained that God had permitted, but not approved, the enslavement of Africans so that they could learn Christianity and the skills of the West in America before returning to Africa to Christianize and civilize Africans. Though proponents of this view often criticized America as materialist, racist, and militaristic, to the extent that they acknowledged the superiority of Western civilization and Christian democracy, they mirrored the dominant national myth.

Another interpretation of black destiny flatly contradicted the myth of the Redeemer Nation. Western civilization, in this view, had been tried and found wanting. The mission of Christianizing the world had passed to others. This argument, as noted in the previous chapter, was most fully articulated by two late nineteenth-century clergymen, Theophilus Gould Steward and James Theodore Holly, both of whom understood the events of their time and scriptural prophecy to mean that the darker peoples of the world would supplant Europeans and Americans in God's design because white Christians had deformed the gospel.

By the end of the nineteenth century, the protest of African-Americans against slavery and racism had evolved several distinct but related themes that challenged the adequacy of the nation's dominant myth. First, blacks asserted that slavery and discrimination were more than aberrations or anomalies in the overall progress of the national destiny; rather, they represented fundamental barriers to the achievement of that destiny. Racism, institutionalized in slavery and segregation, rendered the entire experiment a failure. Second, by criticizing white America, blacks assumed a position of moral authority that made them the true exemplars of Christianity in America. This role was symbolized in the blacks' image of themselves as Israel, which contradicted the metaphor of white America as the New Israel. Third, blacks declared that America was failing its commission to redeem the world. If America would repent and incorporate the Christ-like virtues of the black people in its midst, it might not be too late to construct a just and free civilization. Finally, some concluded that it was indeed already too late. America's apostasy was so great that it would soon be displaced. The long course of Western civilization was finished, and other peoples, "darker peoples," would at last put into practice the gospel to which white Americans had paid no more than lip service.

Starting with an acceptance of the myth of American exceptionalism, black critics in the nineteenth-century pressed toward a theory of history in which American exceptionalism was denied. Oscillating between these two poles, the tradition of black protest registered the degrees of black alienation from the dominant cultural nationalism. At the turn of the twentieth century, when some had lost faith in America or Christianity or both, the mind of much of black America was profoundly ambivalent.

Black protest in the nineteenth century had been predominantly religious. Many of the African-American leaders were ministers. Churches served as major forums for organizing and expressing black grievances, and the primary symbols of protest were religious ones. During the first decades of the twentieth century, new variations on the traditional themes of protest emerged. Though some scholars have claimed that protest was secularized during this period, the black church remained more political and protest more religious than some have thought. The involvement of clergy, for example, in the organization of such "secular" protest organizations as the National Association for the Advancement of Colored People and the Universal Negro Improvement Association, especially on the local level, was extensive. Although neither the NAACP or the UNIA developed any formal relationship with religious bodies, they did justify their goals by appealing to religious ideals. It was republican or civil, rather than biblical religion, however, on which they based their appeal. In its long struggle to desegregate the nation, the NAACP attempted to get the republic to practice its faith by using the guardians of the faith, the courts of law. To the degree it succeeded, the NAACP preserved the religion of the republic for black citizens still denied full participation in the civic rituals of voting and public education.

Marcus Garvey, architect of the largest mass movement black America has ever seen, founded his Universal Negro Improvement Association on the principles of democracy and Christianity, which he hoped to embody in an African republic, a black nation destined to unite the scattered children of Africa around the world. Garvey denied that his movement was antiwhite and professed unwavering faith in the brotherhood of man and the fatherhood of God. Though Garvey and his followers despaired of achieving justice for blacks in America, they remained loyal to the ideals of America and sought to transpose them to their Republic of Africa. Garveyism inspired civic piety among the black masses and structured their piety around symbols appropriate for a black civil religion. The UNIA offered black Americans a cultural nationalism of their own, freed of ambivalence and alienation. To this end, Garvey's movement developed its own hymnal, creed, catechism, and baptismal ritual.

While the Garveyites sought to replace the American civil religion with one of their own, some black Americans began to formulate for themselves an entirely new religioracial identity, divorced from American mythology. Historically, blacks had generally adhered to Christianity while attacking the behavior of white Christians as a travesty of true Christian doctrine. Some, however, found it impossible, in the face of white Christians' racism, to distinguish between true and false Christianity and condemned the entire religion as white man's propaganda. For them, the tension involved in holding the same religion as the oppressor proved too great. Christianity, they asserted, was a religion for whites. In the early twentieth century, esoteric versions of Judaism and Islam laid claim to the allegiance of blacks. In these "new religions" black Americans embraced the alienation forced upon them by the intransigence of racism in Christian America. Spiritually, if not physically, they abandoned America to search for citizenship and acceptance in a different world. Particularly in the Nation of Islam, led by Elijah Muhammed and publicized by Malcolm X, the alienation of black Americans took on mythic form. The black Muslims turned American exceptionalism on its head. American was special all right; America was Satan!

Black protest in the twentieth century, then, has not been as "secular," nor has the black church been as quiescent about protest, as has sometimes been claimed. Black clergy played active roles in the Garvey movement, the NAACP, and in local political affairs, not only in the North, but in the South as well. Granted, much of their political activism would not appear "radical" from the perspective of the 1960s, but protest demonstrations did occur. In 1935, for example, Martin Luther King, Sr., led several thousand black demonstrators on a march from Ebenezer Baptist Church to the city hall of Atlanta in support of voting rights for blacks. And even earlier, the Reverend Adam Daniel Williams, the maternal grandfather of Martin Luther King, Jr., organized rallies at Ebenezer to protest a municipal bond issue that contained no plans for high-school education for black youth. The activism of some black ministers and the legal struggles of the NAACP and the Urban League, lay the groundwork for the movement that began in Montgomery. In this movement, the themes of black religious protest found their most eloquent expression.

As the son, grandson, and great-grandson of Baptist ministers, Martin Luther King, Jr., was deeply rooted in the African-American religious tradition. Though he briefly considered careers in medicine and law, he decided as a teenager that he, too, would enter the ministry. Already, it was apparent that he was, as his father bragged, a magnificent preacher. Throughout the civil rights movement, King instinctively drew upon that black church tradition to inspire the movement's nonviolent wing. He, and others as well, perceived his leadership as fundamentally religious. His style of speaking, the cadence of his voice, the choice of words and images all echoed his church background and evoked, no less than the substance of his message, the rich tradition of black religion. In King, social justice and religion seemed inseparable. It was important that this connection be made, because many whites and some blacks felt that civil rights was really a political not a religious issue. Christian ethics were personal, not social. King was a living contradiction of that position.

His own commitment to social justice came early. Though his childhood was emotionally and economically secure, he personally experienced several instances of discrimination. He was shocked and hurt by them, and like most black children, he never forgot them. During his college years at Morehouse in Atlanta, King began to reflect systematically upon race in America and came to see that racial and economic oppression were linked. He read and re-read Thoreau's "Essay on Civil Disobedience" and appropriated the notion that noncooperation with an evil system is a moral duty. Later, at Crozier Seminary in Pennsylvania, King was influenced by the works of the social gospel advocate, Walter Rauschenbusch, and by Christian ethicists Paul Ramsey and Anders Nygren.[4] By the time he reached maturity, he was deeply convinced that Christianity required Christians to work actively for social justice. His concern for social justice, as well as his intellectual interests, led him to study the social thought of the major Western philosophers as he pursued graduate degrees at Crozier and at Boston School of Theology.

Though strongly attracted to the academic world, King decided that his commitment to social activism for racial justice could best be fulfilled in pastoral ministry in the South. So he accepted the call to pastor the Dexter Avenue Baptist Church in the shadow of the Confederate capitol in Montgomery. As he recalled later, "When I went to Montgomery as a pastor I had not the slightest idea that I would later become involved in a crisis. . . . I neither started the protest nor suggested it. I simply responded to the call of the people for a spokesman."[5] As spokesman for the bus boycott, King hammered out for himself and for the public, hostile and friendly, a philosophy of black protest. The necessity of protest, he proposed, flowed directly from the principle of noncooperation with evil. For black people to endure passively the injustices of segregation was tantamount to cooperating with the system.

Disruptive as demonstrations, marches, rallies, boycotts, and sit-ins were, they were necessary tools for breaking down the complacency of a false social order. Peace in a segregated society was a false peace in which the oppressed merely accepted their subordination out of fear. Black protest didn't create disorder; it revealed the disorder already present in American society, lying just below the surface. To create such tension that whites could no longer ignore the issue of race, to arouse such conflict that whites were forced to negotiate, these were King's goals in city after city, their names a veritable litany of protest: Montgomery, Albany, Birmingham, Washington, Selma, Chicago, Memphis.

To those who argued that the time was not ripe for protest, King replied, "We have waited for more than 340 years for our constitutional and God-given rights" and "we are tired—tired of being segregated and humiliated; tired of being kicked about by the brutal feet of oppression."[6] The time to protest is now. To those who objected that demonstrations encouraged lawlessness, King answered that sometimes allegiance to a higher law required breaking an unjust law and suffering the consequences. Besides, the reaction of whites to black protest revealed the true source of lawlessness. When white police attacked unarmed black demonstrators with clubs, cattle prods, fire hoses, and police dogs, the lawlessness of racism stood revealed, captured on film for the entire nation to see. (And thousands at home and abroad were shocked that such things could happen in America.)

Demonstrations, then, were directed not just at local patterns of discrimination but at racism in the nation at large. Even when they resulted in minimal local gains, they dramatized the plight of blacks in a segregated society and created pressure for change. Moreover, demonstrations were rituals of revival, powerful exhortations to the nation to repent. They were the means for achieving the goal of the movement, at least as King and the Southern Christian Leadership Conference saw it: "to save the soul of the nation." The soul of the nation, King and the demonstrators were saying, with their bodies as well as their words, is tied to the struggle for racial justice. In his most famous defense of protest demonstrations, "Letter from Birmingham Jail," King eloquently restated the relationship between black freedom and the American myth:

> We will reach the goal of freedom in Birmingham and all over the nation, because the goal of America is freedom. Abused and scorned though we may be, our destiny is tied up with America's destiny. Before the pilgrims landed at Plymouth, we were here. Before the pen of Jefferson etched the majestic words of the Declaration of Independence . . . we were here. . . . We will win our freedom because the sacred heritage of our nation and the eternal will of God are embodied in our echoing demands.

King's dream for black Americans was, then, in 1963, still "deeply rooted in the American dream." But just as it had in the nineteenth century, the linkage between African-American destiny and American destiny kept slipping. The fit was not exact. The demonstrators exposed the distance between the ideal image of America and the reality of its failure. In fact, the distance between image and reality was measured precisely by the gap that stretched between black and white America. The demonstrations revealed how wide the separation really was to many Americans who had not even suspected it was there. A gap so wide was bound to call into question the myth of American identity. Was there one America or two?

The society depicted by the demonstrations was not simply divided, it was in conflict. Just as King and the demonstrators intended, their protests brought to the surface the underlying conflict between America's deeds and its principles, and so proved to many Americans for the first time that civil rights was indeed a moral struggle. Aided by men like Bull Connor and Jim Clark, the demonstrations embodied the conflict between good and bad, but in this drama, the old color symbols were reversed. Black was on the side of right and white on the side of wrong. King made it clear: the Ku Klux Klan and White Citizens Councils were "protesting for the perpetuation of injustice," the civil rights activists "for the birth of justice."[8] The demonstrations provoked a crisis of conscience. Americans had to choose, as the freedom song put it, "Which side are you on?" If whites wanted to be on the side of right, they needed to join the cause of blacks. The soul of the nation depended on it.

Once again, the nation was reminded that its destiny lay in the hands of black people. As King told a packed audience on the eve of the Montgomery boycott, "If you will protest courageously, and yet with dignity and Christian love, when the history books are written in future generations, the historians will have to pause and say, There lived a great people—a black people—who injected new meaning and dignity into the veins of civilization. This is our challenge and our overwhelming responsibility." "The Negro," he concluded, "may be God's appeal to this age—an age drifting rapidly to its doom."[9]

According to King, the means blacks had to use to save the nation was nonviolence. "The spiritual power that the Negro can radiate to the world comes from love, understanding, goodwill, and nonviolence."[10] King's first contact with the theory of nonviolence came from reading Thoreau, but a lecture by Mordecai Johnson, president of Howard University, on the life and thought of Mahatma Gandhi inspired King to study the Indian leader and to commit himself to nonviolence. Nonviolence, he thought, was the perfect method for translating the love ethic of Christianity into social reform. With the advice of Bayard Rustin, a black veteran of the Fellowship of Reconciliation, a pacifist organization, King fitted a theory of nonviolent resistance to the tactics of the civil rights movement, although for him nonviolence was far more than a tactic. Along with his conviction that suffering is redemptive, it represented an entire way of life.

King's doctrine of redemptive suffering awakened old themes within African-American religious culture, in particular the theme of the suffering servant, with all its associations in the slave past. The prayers, sermons, and especially the traditional songs "brought to mind the long history of the Negro's suffering," he noted. A simple reference to freedom as the "Promised Land," for example, stirred racial memories and triggered religious emotion. The biblical quotations and allusions that studded King's speeches served to locate the protestors in the long train of prophets and martyrs. The connections between the civil rights movement and the early Christian movement are explicit in King's two epistles in the style of the New Testament, "Letter from Birmingham Jail" and "Paul's Letter to American Christians."[11]

The demonstrations themselves took on the feel of church services. Invariably, they began with rallies in the black churches (which as a consequence became primary targets for white terrorist bombings). These rallies followed a pattern consisting of song, prayer, Scripture reading, discussion of goals and tactics, and an exhortation that frequently sounded like a sermon. From the churches, the demonstrators moved out into the public arena to bear witness with their bodies to the gospel of freedom and equality. Some gave their lives.

Just as in the nineteenth century, black protest in the twentieth claimed that the moral leadership of the nation had passed to blacks. And blacks in both centuries asserted this claim in biblical and messianic terms. Once again the redemptive mission of blacks contradicted the national myth. But this was not to say that African-Americans had simply created a black version of Anglo-Saxonism. King and others realized that there was something universal about the black experience, and they said so. The particular history of black Americans represented the suffering of the poor and oppressed everywhere. And the lesson of black history for the world was that suffering could be redemptive. Nothing expressed this universalistic dimension of black protest as well as the spirituals. King touched on this universalism when he ended his "I have a dream" speech with a vision of the day "when all of God's children, black men and white men, Jews and Gentiles, Protestants and Catholics, will be able to join hands and sing in the words of the old Negro spiritual, 'Free at last! free at last! Thank God Almighty, we are free at last!'"

With King, as with earlier black protest leaders, reflection on black destiny in America seemed inevitably to push beyond the boundaries of America. In part, this was due to his concept of nonviolent love. Love recognized the interrelatedness of all people and impelled one to break down all barriers to community. There is a "network of mutuality" binding all communities, all states, all peoples, King explained to an interfaith committee of ministers who demanded to know why he, an outsider, was demonstrating in Birmingham. "Injustice anywhere is a threat to justice everywhere," he told them.[12] The philosophy of nonviolence tended to corrode the myth of American exceptionalism in King's thinking.

In addition to nonviolence, the independence struggles of

darker peoples around the world influenced King, and many black Americans, to place the civil rights struggle in an internationalist context. As he wrote in 1958,

> This determination of Negro Americans to win freedom from all forms of oppression springs from the same deep longing that motivates oppressed people all over the world. The rumblings of discontent in Asia and Africa are expressions of a quest for freedom and human dignity by people who have long been the victims of colonialism and imperialism. So in a real sense the racial crisis in America is a part of the larger world crisis.[13]

For King, the largest blow against the traditional vision of America's role in the world was delivered by the Vietnam War. Against the wishes of many of his advisors, King began to speak out against the war in 1967. In his most famous antiwar speech, delivered at Riverside Church in New York City exactly one year to the day before his assassination, King described America in terms that Theophilus Gould Steward and James Theodore Holly would have found familiar a century earlier. First, he attacked "the deadly Western arrogance that has poisoned the international atmosphere for so long." Then he accused the nation of being on the wrong side of the revolutions against poverty and injustice taking place all over the world. The only hope for America, he argued, was for the nation "to undergo a radical revolution of values." "We must rapidly begin to shift," he asserted "from a thing-oriented society to a person-oriented society," if the "great triplets of racism, materialism, and militarism" are ever to be conquered.[14]

Finally, King's concern about the relationship between racism and economic injustice, which had troubled him since his youth and which led him to organize the Poor People's Campaign in the last year of his life, caused him to focus increasingly on the need for structural change if the glaring disparity between wealthy and poor were ever to be closed. To attack these problems, a new universalist perspective must prevail, King argued. "Every nation must now develop an overriding loyalty to mankind as a whole." In the "long and bitter—but beautiful—struggle for a new world," everyone dedicated to peace and justice must take on a new role. They must become for Americans the voice of the others—the aliens, the enemies, the poor, the oppressed:

> Beyond the calling of race or nation or creed is this vocation of sonship and brotherhood, and because I believe that the Father is deeply concerned especially for his suffering and helpless and outcast children, I come tonight to speak for them. This I believe to be the privilege and the burden of all of us who deem ourselves bound by allegiances and loyalties which are broader and deeper than nationalism and which go beyond our nation's self-defined goals and positions. We are called to speak for the weak, for the voiceless, for victims of our nation and for those it calls enemy, for no document from human hands can make these humans any less our brothers. . . . Here is the true meaning and value of compassion and nonviolence when it helps us to see the enemy's point of view, to hear his questions, to know his assessment of ourselves. For from his view we may indeed see the basic weakness of our own condition, and if we are mature we may learn and grow and profit from the wisdom of the brothers who are called the opposition.[15]

King came to epitomize the ethical meaning that generations of African-Americans derived from their experience of suffering: an ethics, and nascently a politics, of compassion. The other is not enemy, but rather brother and sister. We must stand in union with the outcast, the wretched of the earth, whoever and wherever they may be. And we, with them, stand in the long line of martyrs, apostles, prophets, and witnesses to the mystery of compassion. "There is no greater love than this, that a man lay down his life for a friend."

Though King attracted widespread support from the local black churches, it was never unanimous. Some clergymen disagreed with his philosophy of social activism because they believed that Christian ethics was a matter of personal morality, not social reform. Society would be changed by obedience to God, not by political agitation. However, the most cogent critic of King's theory of nonviolent resistance came from outside the Christian churches. Malcolm X rejected King's tactics and insisted that blacks use any means necessary to achieve freedom, including violence. Malcolm, and the Nation of Islam for whom he spoke, scorned integration and nonviolence as forms of black self-hatred. Malcolm's critique was made all the more powerful because of his eloquence and integrity. During the last years of King's life, disappointment over the slow pace of change and disillusionment with the tactics of nonviolence led some black activists to adopt a more militant stance and to raise a demand for "black power." For them, King's assassination seemed to seal the demise of nonviolent resistance as a viable means of achieving equality for blacks in America.

In some quarters, the rejection of nonviolence was coupled with strong criticism of the black church as a detriment to black liberation. Integration yielded to goals of liberation, self-determination, and community control. Black pride and the recovery of black cultural identity represented a new mood of independence, some called it separatism, among African-Americans. Black clergy in white churches founded separate black caucuses to deal with questions of black identity and power within white-controlled denominational structures. Responding in part to the militant criticism of the church and in part to their own agenda, black clergy began in the late 1960s and early 1970s to develop a black theology that found God's presence primarily among the poor, the oppressed, and the outcast. It is the voice of these voiceless that black liberation theology seeks to speak.

Entering into dialogue with third world theologians from Latin America, Africa, and Asia, liberation theologians are in a sense the heirs of the vision of Walker, Steward, Holly, King, and the tradition of black religious protest. The continuous tradition of black protest in the United States has by turns called America to live up to its mythic vision of itself, contradicted that image, and argued that an entirely new vision was needed. Some Americans, white as well as black, have over the long years listened to the voices of black protest, realizing, against all appearances, that the nation has need of the wisdom of the invisible men and women, so long enslaved and reviled, if Americans are to recover their ideals, admit their failures, and develop a mature identity as a people. Sadly, many other Americans have looked but have seen nothing, or only distorted images of themselves.

Part II

Under Their Own Vine and Fig Tree

The Black Church

Chapter Four

Richard Allen and the African Church Movement

THE STORY IS A FAMILIAR ONE. On a Sunday morning in 1792 or 1793, the black members of St. George's Methodist Church in Philadelphia learned to their surprise that they could not sit in the benches they normally used. Instead, they were ordered by the sexton to sit upstairs in the gallery recently added at the rear of the church. Though the situation was unfair—they had, after all, contributed like the whites to remodeling the church—they complied with the order. As the opening prayer began, one of the white trustees told Absalom Jones, a respected black parishioner, to get up and move from the front to the back of the gallery. Jones, a dignified man in his late forties, asked the trustee to wait until prayer ended, but the white man insisted he move immediately and motioned for another trustee to help him lift Jones from his knees. As soon as the prayer was over, Jones and the rest of the black worshipers stood and walked out of the church in a body.

So began the movement that resulted in the most important black denomination and arguably the most important African-American institution for most of the nineteenth century, the African Methodist Episcopal Church. As a center for social organization, economic cooperation, educational endeavor, leadership training, political articulation, and religious life, the AME Church exercised unrivaled influence in many black communities. It was for that period the preeminent example of the black church, the one institution that African-Americans controlled. Its history, therefore, and in particular the story of its origins are central to understanding the development and the structures of black community life.

The gallery incident at St. George's is undoubtedly the most famous event in African-American religious history. Because it is such a dramatic and clear-cut example of the racial discrimination that has constantly marred religious life in this country, the story has influenced historians to overemphasize white racism as the reason for the development of the black church. As catalytic as the walkout was, it did not create the black independent church movement in Philadelphia. Long before the disruption, Richard Allen had decided to settle in Philadelphia to "seek and instruct" his "African brethren," whom he described as "a long forgotten people."[1] He had suggested a separate church for the black Methodists of Philadelphia, but his plan was rejected outright by the elder in charge and, at least initially, received little support from the black members of St. George's. Likewise, the leading black citizens of Philadelphia gave Allen no support in this project. They belonged to different denominations and had no interest in establishing a Methodist church. Disappointed, Allen continued to believe that a separate church for blacks was appropriate, as well as necessary. If, as the Methodists proclaimed, all people, regardless of status, were equal in God's sight, then blacks should not only receive the gospel but, once converted, actively preach it. Who better to bring the gospel to the "African brethren" than an "African preacher"? Indeed, the failure of white clerics to evangelize blacks proved to Allen and other early black preachers, that it was their calling to convert and pastor black people.

Allen's primary motive, then, for organizing a separate church was his desire to seek out and instruct "his African brethren," few of whom attended public worship at all. His dream preceded, by as much as six years, the trouble at St. George's. By 1792 the core of a black congregation had already formed out of the membership of the mutual aid association known as the Free African Society. Black religious independence arose from black initiative and not simply in reaction to white discrimination.

Richard Allen was born a slave in Philadelphia, on February 14, 1760, twenty years before the Pennsylvania legislature passed the first emancipation bill in America. He grew to manhood in the era of the Revolution. The rhetoric of individual rights, the spread of Evangelical Christianity, the formation of denominationalism, the gradual abolition of slavery in the North, and increased emancipation in the upper South all influenced the times, the life, and the career of Richard Allen.[2]

As a child, Allen, along with his parents and three siblings, was sold by his owner, Benjamin Chew, the prominent Philadelphia lawyer, to Stokely Sturgis of Kent County, Delaware. Sometime before 1780, Allen experienced the profound inner turmoil and sudden release of religious conversion. By his own account: "I was awakened and brought to see myself, poor, wretched and undone, and without the mercy of God. . . . I cried to the Lord both night and day. . . . all of a sudden my dungeon shook, my chains flew off, and glory to God I cried. My soul was filled. I cried, enough — for me the Saviour died." Conversion led him to take two steps that would shape the rest of his life: he began to "go from house to house, exhorting," and he joined a Methodist class meeting.[3]

Delaware, as well as nearby Maryland and Philadelphia, was a cradle of American Methodism. (Barratt's Chapel erected in 1780 in Allen's own Kent County, was one of the first sites of Methodist organization.) Freeborn Garrettson, Joseph Pilmore, Thomas Coke, Francis Asbury, and other early Methodist itinerants observed that blacks were particularly receptive to John Wesley's heartfelt version of the gospel and urged them to respond to the call for conversion. Blacks joined the first Methodist societies formed in New York City and at Sam's Creek near Frederick,

Maryland, and added their names to the subscription lists for the first Methodist church, erected on John Street in New York in 1768. The direct appeal, dramatic preaching, and plain doctrine of the Methodists, their conscious identification with the "simpler sort," and especially their antislavery beliefs attracted African-Americans, who were gathered into class meetings with whites or organized into all-black classes. Blacks constituted a significant percentage of Methodist growth in the cities of New York, Philadelphia, Baltimore, Charleston, and their environs during the closing decade of the century.

At the time of Allen's conversion and admission into the Methodist society, his master, Sturgis, though himself unconverted, permitted Allen and his oldest brother to attend Methodist meetings every two weeks. Allen later explained that he and his brother deliberately worked harder after conversion in order to disprove the old canard that "religion made worse servants." That piety and work were linked remained a settled conviction in Allen's mind, no doubt because the combination of the two proved so successful in his own life. At Allen's request, Sturgis allowed Methodists to preach in his house. As a result of a sermon delivered by one of them, Freeborn Garrettson, on the text "Thou art weighed in the balance and art found wanting" (with appropriate application to slaveholders), Sturgis decided that slaveholding was wrong. One cannot help but wonder about Allen's role in Sturgis's conversion, since Allen had invited the Methodist preacher. At any rate, in January 1780, Sturgis signed a gradual manumission document agreeing that Allen could hire out his time until he raised sixty pounds in gold or silver or $2,000 in Continental currency to pay for his freedom. In 1781 Allen paid Sturgis $150 as a first installment; it took five more years to pay the last.

Licensed to hire out his time, Allen worked at a variety of jobs during this twilight period between slavery and freedom: he cut wood, did day labor, worked in a brickyard, and drove a salt wagon during the Revolution. All the while he exhorted and preached to those who would listen. After peace was declared, his preaching career began in earnest. Sometimes alone and sometimes in the company of white preachers, Allen traveled widely on the Methodist circuits, preaching, holding prayer meetings, and giving religious counsel to groups of white and black Christians in the small towns and rural settlements of Maryland, Delaware, Pennsylvania, and New York. According to one account, he ranged as far south as South Carolina and even spent two months preaching among Native Americans.[4] Allen's itinerancy between 1780 and 1785 brought him into contact with the founders and early communities of American Methodism. His religious travels gave him experience and a reputation in the developing network of this "plain" church, where a "plain" man could rise and achieve.

In 1785 Bishop Francis Asbury proposed that Allen travel with him on a regular basis, but he laid out certain conditions Allen found unacceptable. In slave counties, Allen would have to avoid contact with slaves and would need to sleep in Asbury's carriage. The question of financial support also gave Allen pause. The bishop might remain unconcerned about temporal affairs, but Allen thought it imprudent for a black preacher to depend solely upon the generosity of others. Rejecting Asbury's offer, he traveled for a while on the Lancaster circuit in Pennsylvania. There he received a call from the elder in charge of St. George's in Philadelphia to preach to the black members of the church. Allen's ministry proved so effective that within a short time he had increased the number of black Methodists by forty-two. Initially he had figured on stopping in Philadelphia for only two weeks, but his success must have persuaded him—and the church elder—that he should stay.

Philadelphia, when Allen settled there, had a black population of 1,600 (almost 6 percent of the city's total). An influx of migrants would increase this number significantly over the next decade, as free blacks and former slaves, like Allen, flocked to the city, primarily from the upper South, in search of work. Though a few blacks, like the sailmaker James Forten, rose to prominence and wealth in Philadelphia, the vast majority supported themselves, as had Allen, in the humbler occupations, as day laborers, teamsters, seamen, mechanics, chimney sweeps, cobblers, tradesmen, and domestics. It was this largely uneducated, poor, and unchurched community Allen sought to instruct. His rapid success at St. George's convinced him that the most effective means to reach them was a separate black church.

Initially, Allen's plan for a separate place of worship attracted only three of the black Methodists of St. George's: Doras Giddings, William White, and Absalom Jones. When approached on the subject, the white elder of St. George's ridiculed the whole idea to Allen's face in "very degrading and insulting language." Rebuffed, Allen and Jones continued to discuss the matter and in 1787 decided to organize a religious society. Motivated, as they put it, by "a love to the people of their complexion whom they beheld with sorrow because of their irreligious and uncivilized state," they intended this Free African Society to function as a benevolent mutual aid organization as well as a nondenominational religious association. This dual aspect of the society was reflected in its rules, which required members to contribute regularly to the common fund for assisting the sick, the widowed, and the orphaned and at the same time obliged them to lead orderly and sober lives, distinguished by temperance, propriety, and marital fidelity.[5]

Surprisingly, within two years Allen had quit the Free African Society. After he rejected several invitations to return, a standing committee formally dismissed him from membership on the grounds that he had stirred up discord by "rashly convening" meetings with members of the society. Allen's motivation for breaking with the society and the charges for dismissing him remain unclear. William Douglass, who abstracted the society's minutes in his *Annals of the First African Church* (1862), speculated that Allen left because "the current of religious sentiment in this Society was not flowing in the direction he desired."[6] Very likely the conflict occurred over religious preferences. Allen wanted to organize a separate black church, preferably Methodist. Apparently his efforts to do so among the membership of the Free African Society met with opposition from those who thought they had formed a nondenominational aid society and wanted to keep it that way. From their perspective, Allen's proselytizing threatened to introduce religious dissension into the society since its members belonged to different denominations and held different beliefs. Their bond of association was philanthropic and moral, "without regard to religious tenets."

After Allen's departure, the Free African Society did move step-by-step toward becoming an African church, avoiding the divisive issue of denominational identity as long as possible. In addition to guarding the morals of its members, the society began to take on the functions of a religious congregation. Members, for example, could choose to have their marriages solemnized in a wedding ceremony developed by the society, and in January 1791 the society initiated regular meetings for Sabbath worship. As they evolved into a church community, the members of the Free African Society came face-to-face with two practical problems: they needed a regular place for worship, and they needed to agree upon some form of religious discipline and doctrine. In search of a permanent meetinghouse, they turned to the prominent physician and philanthropist Benjamin Rush for assistance and advice. Rush not only sympathized with their desire for an African church but offered to draft for them a plan of church government and articles of faith general enough "to embrace all, and yet so orthodox in cardinal points to offend none."[7] In the summer of 1791, the majority of the members voted to accept Rush's outline of church organization. The transformation from aid society to congregation was, at least in theory, complete. All that was lacking was a minister and a building.

At this point the gallery incident at St. George's galvanized the black Methodists—indeed, the black community at large—into action. The walkout from St. George's made the need to erect a separate church not only apparent but urgent. The Free African Society took the lead in the campaign to raise funds for the church. Though a few members refused to allow their dues to be used for this enterprise, the majority approved the transfer of their money from the society to a church building fund. Now that his goal was shared by the majority, Richard Allen joined the common task. He and Absalom Jones, William White, and William Witcherly, all active members of the Free African Society, constituted the committee assigned the task of finding property and raising more funds for a church building. Again with the aid of Benjamin Rush, and also of Robert Ralston, a wealthy white merchant, they quickly compiled a list of white and black subscribers. The white Methodist elder opposed the project and threatened to dismiss all the black Methodists who did not erase their names from the subscription lists. Allen and the others replied that they had not violated the Methodist discipline and argued that the disgraceful treatment they suffered at St. George's more than justified their efforts to build a church of their own.

Though interrupted by the yellow fever epidemic that struck the city in 1793, the campaign succeeded and the committee authorized Allen to purchase a lot on the corner of Lombard and Sixth Streets. After Allen had reached an agreement with the seller, the rest of the committee decided to buy a different lot on Fifth Street, leaving him personally responsible for the first lot, which would eventually become the site of Mother Bethel Church. As the originator of the idea of an African church, Allen was given the honor of breaking ground for construction. With the church building underway, the leaders of the church, called "elders and deacons" under their ecumenical plan of church government, now faced the issue of denominational affiliation.

According to Allen, the majority favored the Methodists, but the local elder continued to refuse to have anything to do with an African church. Methodist policy dictated that the ordinances of Baptism and the Lord's Supper could only be administered by an ordained elder or deacon. In 1793 the only black preacher in Philadelphia was Allen, but he was not ordained. To whom, then, could these blacks turn for full ministerial service and denominational legitimacy? The majority of the church leaders voted to affiliate with the Episcopalians. Perhaps their choice was influenced by the active concern of the Reverend Joseph Pilmore, the Episcopal rector of St. Paul's Church, who had demonstrated his willingness to minister to black Philadelphians by presiding at their weddings and by assisting in the religious organization of the Free African Society. At any rate, only two leaders voted to remain Methodist, Jones and Allen. On August 12, 1794, the African Church of Philadelphia "consented and committed all ecclesiastical affairs to the Protestant Episcopal Church of America" and two years later incorporated as St. Thomas's Episcopal Church with 246 members. Allen said he was approached about pastoring the church but declined because he was committed to Methodism. Absalom Jones, despite his Methodist sympathies, accepted the pastorate and eventually was ordained as the first black Episcopal priest in the United States. Allen and Jones, denominational differences aside, remained friends and collaborated on several projects during the following years.

Although the majority, including his oldest supporters, Jones and White, affiliated with the Episcopal Church, Allen remained single-minded in pursuit of his goal. On May 5, 1794, he and eleven other black Methodists met at his home to make final plans for a separate house of worship. They agreed to purchase a frame structure, a former blacksmith shop, and move it to the lot Allen had purchased at Sixth and Lombard. Carpenters were hired to make the building suitable for church meetings, and by July, Allen had the satisfaction of watching Bishop Asbury dedicate Bethel African Church. On April 9, 1799, the year before the Methodist General Conference approved ordination of blacks, Asbury ordained Allen as a local deacon.

Bethel increased in membership during its first decade, assisted by a general revival among Methodists in Philadelphia, which Allen reported to Asbury in February 1798: "Our churches are crowded, particularly Bethel. We are now making more seats, and think shortly we must enlarge the house. It is at Bethel the work is most general."[8] In 1799 the Methodists reported 211 black members and 411 whites in Philadelphia; by June 1803 Allen informed an English correspondent that Bethel had 457 members. The frame church, no longer adequate, was replaced by a rough-cast brick structure in 1805.

It took eight years, but Allen had realized his dream: the African Methodists had their own place of worship. His decision to stay with the Methodists, despite all obstacles, was based on his conviction that Methodist simplicity was better suited to the evangelization of an unlettered people than the more "highflown" instruction offered by the Episcopalians and Presbyterians. From personal experience, as a convert and as a preacher, he felt certain that the plain gospel presented in spiritual (i.e., extemporaneous) preaching would warm many more hearts than would manuscript sermons, crafted in the preacher's study. Moreover, he prized the Methodist system of discipline as an effective method of reforming and ordering the lives of individuals and groups. By means of small class meetings, Methodists simultaneously encouraged individual participation and communal coercion. In this way, values became internalized. The life that these intimate communities sanctioned was supposed to be simple, honest, modest, provident, and sober. This set of virtues, implied by the term "discipline," appealed to Allen personally and as a method for lifting a "lowly" people "up from slavery." Methodism offered the masses of black people a coherent pattern of values by which they could order their lives. The Methodist way provided a detailed prescription of how one should live, supplied communities to observe and encourage one's moral progress, and reinforced one's commitment to a virtuous life by emotional praying, preaching, and revival meetings.

Allen's own career demonstrated the value of Methodist doctrine and discipline for black people. The Methodists had preached the gospel that emancipated him spiritually from sin and physically from slavery. For Allen, piety, discipline, and freedom constituted a distinctive Methodist ethos, a gospel of equality for blacks and whites alike. Therefore, when he observed Methodist preachers dismissing black members from society without trial, for trivial offenses and on the basis of hearsay evidence, he accused them of acting "without discipline." Their racial prejudice and authoritarianism betrayed the Methodist faith. In his later years, looking back over the history of American Methodists, Allen remarked on their declension: "The simplicity of the Gospel that was among them is not now apparent" and their "discipline is altered considerably from what it was." He, and generations of African Methodists to follow, believed that it was the vocation of Bethel to preach the simplicity of the gospel and the discipline of Methodism, from which white Methodists had strayed. "We would ask for the good old way, and desire to walk therein," he confessed simply.[9]

The most obvious example of Methodist backsliding was the retreat of the General Conference from firm antislavery legislation in the face of southern resistance. Closer to home, the efforts of white elders to control Bethel further alienated black Methodists from denominational authority. In 1796 Bethel had been incorporated under the Methodist conference, thus placing the church property under the control of the local elder appointed by the conference. Ezekiel Cooper, a white Methodist, drew up the papers of incorporation in this manner, despite the wishes of the Bethelites, because it was Methodist policy. The congregation first learned of the matter ten years later when James Smith, a newly appointed elder, demanded the church keys and books and forbade any meetings not called by him. When the Bethelites refused to comply and protested that the church was theirs, he told them that it belonged to the conference and threatened to dismiss them from the Methodist society. A quick appeal to an attorney revealed that Smith was right. But all was not lost, the lawyer informed them. A vote of two-thirds of the membership could amend the terms of incorporation. Accordingly, in 1807 the congregation, men and women, unanimously passed a supplement that gave the black trustees control of the church property and went even farther in granting them the right to nominate "any duly qualified person to officiate in place of the elder" in case the elder of St. George's neglected to minister at Bethel regularly.[10] Finally, the supplement restricted the elder of St. George's from assigning anyone to preach at Bethel unless the majority of Bethel trustees concurred with his choice.

A succession of elders at St. George's contested the legality of this "African Supplement." They ignored its provisions, overcharged for their services, neglected to supply regular preaching, failed to acknowledge the authority of Bethel committees to discipline their own members, and even attempted to put the church property up for sale. To pressure the congregation to yield, one elder forbade all preachers to serve Bethel under pain of dismissal, published a circular disowning the Bethelites as Methodists, and opened a rival African church to draw away members. When all these steps failed the elder, Robert Roberts, insisted on taking spiritual charge of Bethel and announced that he would preach from its pulpit whether the trustees approved or not. On the Sunday he planned to preach, the congregation denied him access to the pulpit by blocking the aisles. Another elder tried a different approach: he sued for legal control of Bethel. After a long and expensive suit, the Pennsylvania Supreme Court decided in favor of the African congregation.

Black Methodists of Bethel Church in Baltimore, themselves locked in a similar struggle with white authorities, reacted enthusiastically to the news from Philadelphia. On January 21, 1816, their leader, Daniel Coker, preached a celebratory sermon comparing the victory of the Philadelphia brethren to the return of the Jews from captivity in Babylon. Contact with Coker in Baltimore and reports of conflicts between black and white Methodists in several other locales persuaded Allen to issue a call for a convention of African Methodists to meet in Philadelphia to discuss their common problems. In April, delegates representing the black Methodists of Baltimore, Wilmington, Attleborough, Pennsylvania, and Salem, New Jersey, gathered in response to Allen's call. Sizable black congregations in New York City and Charleston, South Carolina, did not send delegations but followed the proceedings with interest. The convention delegates "in order to secure their privileges and promote union and harmony among themselves" resolved that the churches they represented "should become one body, under the name of the African Methodist Church."[11]

As the leaders of the two largest churches and as men of exceptional ability, Allen and Coker seemed the logical choices to lead the new denomination. Before a vote could be taken, Allen was called away from the convention on personal business; during his absence, the delegates elected him and Coker the first bishops of the AME Church. Upon his return, Allen accepted the election of Coker but objected that the new church was too small to justify two bishops. The public would think them ambitious for status and power. Persuaded by his remarks, the delegates reversed themselves and elected just one bishop, Richard Allen. On April 11, 1816, seventeen years after Asbury had ordained him a local deacon, the fifty-six-year-old Allen was consecrated bishop by the imposition of hands of five ordained ministers, including those of his old friend, Absalom Jones.

The next step was to formulate the rules and structure of the new church. Allen, Coker, and James Champion, an officer in Allen's congregation, modeled the by-laws of the African Methodist Episcopal Church upon the discipline of the Methodists, with two exceptions. They abolished the office of presiding elder and restored the legislation prohibiting slaveholders from membership. To the first edition of the AME Discipline (1817), they added a historical preface that explained the cause of their separation from the white Methodists:

> We have deemed it expedient to have a form of Discipline, whereby we may guide our people in the fear of God, in the unity of the Spirit, and in the bonds of peace, and preserve us from that spiritual despotism which we have so recently experienced—remembering, that we are not to Lord it over God's heritage, as greedy dogs, that can never have enough; but with long suffering, and bowels of compassion, to bear each other's burdens, and so fulfil the law of Christ.[12]

The AME convention of 1816 occurred within the context of general denominational ferment in the early nineteenth century. Federal and state disestablishment of religion created an environment of voluntarism in which church organization flourished. Between 1790 and 1810, African Baptists, Methodists, Presbyterians, and Episcopalians, concluding that religious freedom applied to them, too, founded churches, asserted congregational control, and struggled for autonomy from white elders, bishops, and associations. The African Methodists were the first to achieve independent control of church property, finances, ministry, and governance on the denominational level. Between 1815 and 1821, they organized three separate denominations: the Union Church of Africans, organized by Peter Spencer in Wilmington, Delaware; Allen's African Methodist Episcopal Church; and the African Methodist Episcopal Zion Church, founded in New York City in 1821. From bitter experience, these black Methodists had learned that congregational independence was precarious as long as they remained under the ecclesiastical jurisdiction of whites.

Denominational organization freed Bethel from meddling white elders and at the same time burdened Allen with new responsibilities as bishop of a rapidly expanding church. In 1817 the AME organizational structure consisted of two annual conferences (regional districts), in Philadelphia and Baltimore, served by seven itinerant ministers. In 1826 there were three annual conferences, seventeen itinerant ministers, and ten circuits; and membership, which had stood at 6,784 in 1818, had grown to 7,937. (The total would have been 3,000 more but for the suppression of the AME Church in Charleston after the discovery of the Denmark Vesey conspiracy.) By 1827 AME missionaries had crossed the Alleghenies to preach in Ohio, émigrés from Mother Bethel had established St. Peter's AME Church in Haiti, and four AME missions had been founded in Canada. In 1828 the sixty-eight-year-old Allen finally received some administrative help when Morris Brown, former pastor of the Charleston church, was consecrated as the second bishop of the AME Church.

Interdenominational squabbles and church politics harassed Allen's entire ministry. Black Methodists in Wilmington and New York, for example, rejected his overtures and decided to go their own way. Though Peter Spencer, leader of the Wilmington church, participated in the Philadelphia convention in 1816, he never affiliated with Allen, perhaps because his own organization antedated Allen's by a year. In addition, Spencer disapproved of the AME church structure, particularly the episcopate. Black

Methodists in New York organized a separate church in 1796 but failed to send representatives to Philadelphia, perhaps because of intercity rivalry between the two black communities. In 1820 several leaders of the New York Zion Church began to negotiate with Allen in secret. But when Allen precipitously invaded their territory by sending one of his elders to organize a society in New York, the Zionites felt betrayed. Allen alienated them further when he refused their request to ordain some of their men unless they first agreed to place themselves under his conference. To the Zionites, Allen seemed ambitious and opportunistic. To Allen, no doubt, the Zionites seemed divisive, at a time when the strength of the black churches depended on unity. The New York Methodists could take some comfort, however, from the fact that a group of dissidents from Bethel set up a rival church only ninety feet from Allen's and proceeded to affiliate with the Zionites. When the trustees of Bethel and Wesley, as the new church was called, attempted a rapprochement and invited Allen to preach at the Wesley pulpit, a near riot ensued. As Allen preached, one of the Wesley partisans sat on the pulpit, interrupted the sermon, and even spat on the bishop. Eventually the two churches were involved in a lawsuit, which Bethel lost.

On the one hand, these internecine squabbles must have troubled Allen and distracted him from more urgent concerns. On the other hand, the tendency of black, no less than white, Protestants to "multiply by division" demonstrated the vitality and diversity of their church life and their determination to exercise religious independence. From one perspective, three distinct African Methodist denominations may seem redundant; from another, these church and denominational disagreements may be seen as part of the process by which free blacks organized their communities.

As a successful and respected figure, Allen aroused his share of jealousy and animosity. In 1823, for example, he was attacked in print by Jonathan Tudas, a disgruntled former member of Bethel (and leader in the founding of Wesley), who published a pamphlet charging that Allen mishandled church funds during his tenure as treasurer. Tudas also accused Allen of stirring up racial tension by publicly criticizing whites and suggested that the whole incident at St. George's had been invented, or at least misrepresented, for Allen's own purposes. On behalf of Allen, the trustees of both Bethel and Wesley published a rebuttal, *The Sword of Truth*, in which they portrayed Tudas as a malcontent who had stirred up trouble at St. Thomas's African Episcopal Church, created dissension at Bethel, disrupted Wesley, and finally quit the church to avoid trial for "seducing a poor white woman."[13] Tudas's charges must have been particularly galling to Allen, since he had for years accepted no salary from Bethel and had, in fact, frequently paid church debts out of his own pocket. Tudas's attack had to be rejected in the strongest terms possible, not just because it defamed Allen, but because it defamed the AME Church, which the public identified with Allen. Though the AMEs had other leaders, like Coker and Brown, the AME Church was the church of Allen; he was the founder. More important, his life exemplified the values and goals of the church: in a phrase, the independent Christian "manhood" to which the race should aspire.

Allen's leadership rested upon his role as pastor and on his status as a successful businessman. Ecclesiastical and civic authority were intertwined in Allen's career, but not because the church was the only civic institution blacks controlled. In his own thinking Allen made a direct link between freedom and piety, prosperity and morality. He had achieved freedom and prosperity, under God's providence, of course, by dint of honesty, industry, discipline, and responsibility. Just as these values had raised him from slavery, so they could raise the black race from poverty and degradation. Though born in bondage, Allen had prospered enough (as proprietor of blacksmithing, shoemaking, and chimney-sweeping businesses) to buy several income properties and to build a three-story brick house in which more than a few white bishops and elders enjoyed his hospitality. All the while he ministered to his flock, he also worked, so that with the help of his first wife, Flora, and his second, Sarah, he never had to depend upon the Bethel congregation for support. In fact, when it came time to die, he was able to leave his widow and six children an estate valued at $80,000. Allen was justifiably proud, as he remarked late in life, that "my hands administered to my necessities."[14]

The social and racial dimensions, however, are what made Allen's ethic much more than a gospel of wealth. It was not enough to merely refrain from debauchery, folly, and idleness. It was not enough to provide for one's family. True Christians had to stretch out their hands beyond the circle of family and friends to comfort the poorer neighbor, the stranger, the widow, and the orphan. The corporal and spiritual works of mercy fulfilled Christ's most fundamental command and at the same time refined the spirit, freeing Christians from the weight of possessions. Individual acts of charity, however, did not suffice. Given the poverty and illiteracy of blacks in Philadelphia and elsewhere, charity needed to be institutionalized. Allen helped found the Free African Society, the Bethel Benevolent Society, and the African Society for the Education of Youth precisely to institutionalize compassion. These self-help and moral reform societies also served as outlets of race pride and community action. Though he did not hesitate to ask white philanthropists, like Rush, for occasional help, Allen knew that blacks themselves had to cooperate to change the day-to-day conditions in which they lived. Racial progress depended upon moral reform and education. Without thrift, temperance, industry, fidelity, and responsibility, blacks could not climb out of poverty.

Allen also recognized that race advancement was blocked by white stereotypes about blacks. Statistics on crime, poverty, even disease, in the free black community were used to argue that blacks were unfit for freedom. Therefore, blacks had to lead moral and sober lives in order to disprove racist theories of black inferiority:

> Much depends upon us for the help of our color—more than many are aware. If we are lazy and idle, the enemies of freedom plead it as a cause why we ought not to be free, and say we are better in a state of servitude, and that giving us our liberty would be an injury to us; and by such conduct we strengthen the bands of oppression and keep many in bondage who are more worthy than ourselves. I entreat you to consider the obligations we lie under to help forward the cause of freedom.[15]

The antislavery cause required free blacks to organize for moral uplift in order to demonstrate that they were capable of freedom and were not innately inferior. Allen was well aware of the absurdity of trying to prove that persons were capable of freedom, especially in the city that had in his own lifetime declared that all people were equal and endowed with the inalienable right of liberty. He protested that white attitudes blamed the victim for the crime:

> The Judicious part of mankind, will think it unreasonable, that a superior good conduct is looked for from our race, by those who stigmatize us as men whose baseness is incurable and may therefore be held in a state of servitude that a merciful man would not doom a beast to; yet you try what you can to prevent our rising from a state of barbarism you represent us to be in; but we can tell you, from a degree of experience that a black man, although reduced to the most abject state human nature is capable of . . . can think, reflect and feel injuries. . . . We believe if you would try the experiment of taking a few black children, and cultivate their minds with the same care and let them have the same prospect in view as to living in the world, as you would wish for your own children, you would find upon the trial, they were not inferior in mental endow-

ments. . . . Will you, because you have reduced us to the unhappy condition our color is in plead our incapacity for freedom . . . as a sufficient cause for keeping us under the grievous yoke?[16]

Allen was forced to protest again when prominent newspaper editor and publisher Matthew Carey attacked the black people of Philadelphia for their behavior during the yellow fever epidemic of 1793. Carey had written a pamphlet claiming that black Philadelphians profited from the epidemic by charging exorbitant fees for assisting the sick and by outright stealing from the homes of the deceased. Though Carey had praised Allen and Jones personally for their devoted service to the sick and dying, in their view he had libeled the black community. In their own *Narrative of the Proceedings of the Black People during the Late Awful Calamity in Philadelphia*, they tried to set the record straight by recounting frequent instances of blacks voluntarily tending the ill and burying the dead even after it had been proven that black people were not immune to the disease, as had been thought. Carey's attack was not only wrong, it was dangerous because it fed white prejudice against free blacks.

A far greater threat to free blacks, not only in Philadelphia but everywhere in the nation, appeared with the establishment of the American Colonization Society in 1817. The ACS, a reform society, was organized to support the emigration of free blacks from America to Africa. Its members believed that emigration would solve the problem of slavery by removing one of the major obstacles to abolition: the anomalous presence of free blacks in a country belonging to whites. Allen and other black leaders feared that the ACS would pressure Congress into legislating the emigration of all free blacks, thus resolving the slavery problem by expelling the most vociferous opponents of the system. Two weeks after the organization of the ACS, a mass protest meeting was held at Bethel. Initially, Allen did not object to voluntary emigration for blacks. Indeed, along with James Forten, he supported the plans of Paul Cuffe, a black ship captain from Massachusetts and an early advocate of colonization in Africa. Moreover, the AME Church supported missionary enterprise.in Africa and the Caribbean. Daniel Coker sailed as a missionary to Sherbro, West Africa, on a voyage supported by the ACS in 1820. Responding to Haitian President Boyer's invitation to U.S. blacks to emigrate, several members of Bethel, presumably with Allen's blessing, settled in Haiti in 1824.

But Allen strongly opposed the notion that blacks must leave this land to find freedom. As debate over the desirability of emigration continued to divide the black community, Allen came to see colonization as a mistake and publicized his view in the November 2, 1827, issue of *Freedom's Journal*, the first black newspaper in the United States. First he questioned the colonizationists' plan to use African-Americans to civilize and convert Africans. Since American blacks were largely illiterate and uneducated, how could anyone argue that they were ready to convert or civilize others? They desperately needed education and religious instruction themselves. The real purpose of the colonizationists, he warned, was to remove free blacks from the country so that slaves would not see other blacks enjoying liberty. Furthermore, Allen wondered, if there were enough land and labor for the thousands of immigrants flocking to America each year, why send "the first tillers of the land" away? Finally, he appealed to patriotism: "This land, which we have watered with our tears and our blood, is now our mother country and we are well satisfied to stay where wisdom abounds, and the gospel is free." If reformers were sincere about ridding the nation of slavery, they should abandon illusory schemes of colonization, support the education and advancement of blacks here, and oppose slavery in the South. Allen believed that well-intentioned blacks who supported colonization were flirting with catastrophe.

One of the strongest arguments against colonization in Allen's mind was the fear that the large-scale emigration of free blacks would effectively abandon the vast majority of American blacks to slavery. Without the activism of free blacks in the North, the antislavery movement would be weak indeed. The arrival of recently freed slaves from the South and of free blacks from South Carolina following Vesey's conspiracy reminded Allen and the Bethel congregation of slavery's harsh reality. The Bethel Church basement and the Allen home sheltered fugitive slaves en route to points further North, out of reach of slave catchers. Allen himself was accosted by a slave catcher who swore that he was a runaway slave. But Allen had resided in Philadelphia for more than twenty years and was so well known that the constable serving the warrant was embarrassed to ask him to appear before the magistrate. Allen sued the slave speculator, whom the magistrate remanded to jail when he failed to post an $800 bond. Three months in jail was long enough to teach the man a lesson, Allen concluded, and he dropped the charges. While Allen's prominence saved him from kidnapping, less famous blacks had more to fear.

In 1794 Allen published *An Address to Those Who Keep Slaves*, in which he attacked slavery and the arguments for it. Pointing out "the dreadful insurrections" slaves had mounted as proof that they were far from content, he warned slaveholders: "If you love your children, if you love your country, if you love the God of love, clear your hands from slaves, burden not your children with them." Turning to the slaves, Allen advised them to trust in God and avoid despair. Based upon his own experience of enslavement, he cautioned that impatience only led to emotional "darkness and perplexity." Religion could help the slaves in two ways. It might lead to a relationship of mutual regard between master and slave, a relationship that would tend to promote the liberty of the slave, just as it had for Allen. And in those situations in which reciprocity between master and slave was impossible, religion would instill in the heart of the slave a freedom no master could take away: the freedom of the children of God.[17]

Fugitive slave laws, slave catchers, the American Colonization Society, and legal and customary discrimination clearly demonstrated to free blacks that their situation was tenuous and seemed to be worsening with each passing decade. They would have to organize some general protest, some national movement to fight back. At the initiative of Hezekiah Grice, a free black from Baltimore who had circulated a letter to black leaders calling for a national convention, Allen and the Philadelphia leaders issued a public notice of a convention to be held in 1830, the first of the national Negro conventions. Forty people attended the 1830 convention, whose sessions were held at Bethel September 20–24, with Allen sitting as president and convenor. The convention organized the American Society of Free Persons of Colour, whose purpose was to improve conditions for blacks in the United States and establish a settlement in Canada for those driven from their homes by discriminatory laws. In addition, the convention published an address to free people of color, urging them to "pursue all legal means for the speedy elevation of ourselves and brethren to the scale and standing of men." To achieve this end, the convention recommended racial unity, self-help, and a practical program encouraging agriculture and mechanical arts. Agriculture, black leaders reasoned, would lead to independence, and mechanical arts would "ennoble the mind"; both, they confidently predicted, would eventually "give us the standing and condition we desire."[18]

When the convention met, Allen was seventy years old; he died within the year, at the age of seventy-one. The convention represented a fitting conclusion to his career. From an unordained preacher struggling to start an African church and facing rejection from the leaders of black Philadelphia, Allen had become one of the foremost black leaders in the nation, the bishop of one of the earliest black denominations, and the president of the first black political organization. Allen had single-mindedly pursued his course and more often than not succeeded. How can we account for his record of leadership? Allen did not question that it was his responsibility to lead, to make pronouncements, to take positions on issues and publish them, to represent and defend the race. Though he was certainly not timid and could seem opinionated, his leadership, because it was basically religious, remained pastoral. One does not sense in Allen the pride or self-absorption of the autocrat. His prose style and his portrait reveal a plain and straightforward man—assured, sober, authentic.

An incident in Allen's youth is a key to his character. While living in Delaware, he found a trunk filled with money and advertised for its owner, returning the trunk with its contents intact. Allen refused the money pressed upon him as a reward, and when the owner insisted on giving him a suit of fine clothes, Allen relented but only if the suit were made of plain cloth. The Methodist discipline itself enjoined "extravagance in useless ornaments and unnecessary fashionable dress": Allen traced the declension of Methodism to the introduction of the ministerial gown, an affectation from the Church of England. His insistence on simplicity was an essential factor in his leadership and explains his ability, despite his prosperity and success, to remain close to the situation of his church members. Because he did so, the pattern of his life could remain an effective exemplar for them; his way seemed possible for them too. Thus Allen's life, as much if not more than his sermons, preached the plain gospel he saw as the essence of Methodism and the salvation of his people.

Chapter Five

The Black Church: Continuity within Change

DURING THE PAST FIFTY YEARS, sweeping economic, political, social, and cultural changes have profoundly affected the religious institutions of black Americans. Migration, urbanization, and the civil rights movement, to mention only the most obvious examples of large-scale social change, have fundamentally altered the conditions of life for African-Americans. In this context, the church has served both as a source of stability and as a vehicle of change. By conserving traditional religious culture, black churches gave black communities and individuals a significant sense of continuity with the past. By evoking familiar religious symbols to interpret novel circumstances, black pastors helped their people to accommodate disruptions caused by rapid change. As the mention of civil rights suggests, the churches not only reacted to social and political change; they also participated in bringing it about. In addition to external factors, internal theological, liturgical, and institutional developments have been major sources of change in black religious life over the past five decades.

For most of that period, the "great migration" of African-Americans, which began around World War I, continued to shift the black population from rural areas to urban centers, and from South to North. While the Depression slowed migration during the 1930s, between 1940 and 1970, 4.4 million black southerners left the South, with the vast majority settling in northern and, to a lesser extent, western cities. Even those blacks who remained in the South (never less than 52 percent of the total black population) moved in ever increasing numbers to cities.[1] This massive movement of people disrupted congregations, transplanted religious customs, taxed the resources of urban churches, and formed, in the burgeoning ghettos, favorable conditions for religious innovation.

Facing an unfamiliar urban environment, rural migrants looked to the church to reaffirm the traditional values and communal ties that had always given them a sense of social location back home. In some instances they joined already established churches; in others they founded new ones of their own. The sheer number of migrants enlarged the membership of existing churches and tested their capacities to absorb the new arrivals. In the early years of the migration, some churches were so overcrowded that they had to hold double services. As the migrants continued to flood in by the thousands, pastors and church boards embarked on extensive and expensive building programs to increase the seating capacity of their buildings. Some churches established social auxiliaries to assist the migrants. Abyssinian Baptist in New York, Olivet Baptist in Chicago, and First Congregational in Atlanta, for example, conducted employment bureaus, day-care centers, kindergartens, adult education classes, drama groups, orchestras, social clubs, athletic events, and various youth programs, even in the depths of the Depression.[2]

While some of the newcomers took pride in the size and prestige of the large city churches, others missed the intimacy and status they had enjoyed in smaller churches "down home." Differences in educational and economic levels and in styles of worship distinguished migrants from some long-time residents and from each other. These disparities, as well as the usual divisiveness of church politics, splintered congregations and multiplied the number of churches in urban black neighborhoods. The proliferation of congregations, many of them so poor and so small that they had to gather in storefronts or homes for worship, prompted the popular remark that ghettos had at least one church on every block and led some sociologists to wonder whether the black community was "overchurched."[3]

Besides increasing the size and number of urban black churches, migration also increased the variety of black religious life by exposing people to new religious options. Accustomed to deciding between Baptist, Methodist, and perhaps Holiness-Pentecostal churches back home, migrants to the cities encountered black Jews, black Muslims, black Spiritualists, and the disciples of a host of charismatic religious figures like Father Divine and Daddy Grace, to name two of the most famous. In the cities black Protestants came into contact with Roman Catholicism, usually for the first time, since Catholics had been scarce in the rural South except for lower Louisiana and Maryland, the traditional centers of black Catholic population. From 1940 to 1975, there was a dramatic increase in the number of black Catholics.[4]

Another intensive movement of people, this time from beyond our national borders, made a new and surprising contribution to the religious variety of urban America. Immigrants from Puerto Rico, Cuba, and more recently, Haiti, have introduced the traditional gods of Africa to the United States. Over the past two decades, the religions of Santería and Voodoo, which originated during slavery in Cuba and Haiti respectively, have spread to black and Hispanic communities across the country. Here, as in Cuba and Haiti, initiates celebrated the feasts of the gods in rituals of drumming, singing, and dancing that derived ultimately from West and Central Africa. Underlying these rituals was the belief that the gods rule over all aspects of life. By offering them praise and sacrifice, people attracted their favor and activated their powerful intercession in times of illness or misfortune. In ceremonies of spirit possession, entranced mediums made personal contact between gods and humans possible by embodying the god for the community. Whenever something inexplicably went wrong, priest-diviners determined the cause and prescribed the means for setting things right. In these ways, Santería and Voodoo preserved a view of life as personal and relational in the midst of a society that seemed increasingly impersonal and atomistic.

Although the number of North American blacks that converted to these religions was small, the number of their adherents, according to news reports, was growing. In the 1960s reawakened interest in the African heritage prompted some African-Americans to adopt African names, styles of dress, and religious traditions. In 1970 one group of black Americans went so far as to establish an "African" village in South Carolina patterned on the culture of the Yoruba people of Nigeria. Yoruba and Yoruba-derived religious communities in Nigeria, Cuba, Brazil, and the United States recently established formal links with one another by instituting annual "Orisa Tradition" conferences (*orisa* being the Yoruba word for the gods). The third conference was held in 1986 in New York City.[5]

Historical studies of twentieth-century black religion have emphasized the dichotomy between "mainline" established churches and storefront congregations in urban black communities. The former were supposedly middle-class bastions of traditional Protestantism, while the latter housed the esoteric sects and cults preferred by the lower classes. It is important to remember, however, that numerous storefront churches were Baptist and Methodist missions, newly formed congregations too poor to afford a regular church building. The stereotypical contrast between the ecstatic worship of the storefront and the sedate liturgy of the mainline church has been overdrawn. Mainline churches provided a greater variety of musical and liturgical styles than has been recognized. Significant theological and liturgical differences did divide black churches during this period, but they did not conform neatly to the storefront-mainline model or to the church-sect typology.[6]

One of the most significant theological and liturgical developments over the past fifty years was the growth of the Holiness-Pentecostal family of churches into one of the largest denominational groups, alongside Baptist and Methodists, in black America. Contrary to Baptist and Methodist doctrine, Holiness and Pentecostal evangelists preached an experience subsequent to conversion called baptism of the Holy Spirit, which was attested, they claimed, by reception of the Spirit's gifts of healing, teaching, prophesying, discernment of spirits, and especially speaking in tongues. Since the Spirit's gifts empowered women no less than men, Holiness and Pentecostal churches proved much more willing to accept women as pastors than did the Methodists or the Baptists, though the majority of their pastors and elders remained male. Their emphasis upon the literal experience of the Spirit's power encouraged Holiness-Pentecostal worshipers to manifest their religious emotions in ecstatic displays of shouting, singing, and dancing that elicited the pejorative nickname "holy rollers" from those who favored a more sedate liturgy. By introducing the use of guitars, pianos, and drums in church music, the Holiness-Pentecostal congregations significantly affected the development of black gospel music and gradually influenced the musical tastes of churches that once banned such instruments as tools of the devil. The sanctified churches, as they were also called, required their members to observe a strict moral ethic that prohibited tobacco, alcohol, narcotics, gambling, and "worldly" entertainment. In effect, the sanctified churches themselves constituted little social realms in which the music and ecstasy of religious worship afforded tired and downtrodden people a recreative catharsis that helped them face the oppressive and frequently hostile outside world. The values inculcated in the lives of the sanctified church members—honesty, thrift, hard work, and discipline, combined with the moral asceticism mentioned above—structured their daily lives around a coherent system of beliefs and, within the limits of racial discrimination, tended to promote upward mobility.[7]

Social critics have complained that the proliferation of black churches fragmented the black community into competing sects. If only they had overcome their differences, the argument goes, black churches might have pooled their resources and become an effective force for the economic and social development of the black community. Perhaps so, but the fact remains that individual ministers and churches did cooperate to better the condition of the race. During the 1930s, for example, ministers in Harlem organized "Don't buy where you can't work" boycotts against stores and agencies that refused to hire black employees (anticipating Operation Breadbasket and PUSH by thirty years). It should be noted that their efforts, though rarely successful, depended upon a well-established network of cooperation between black ministers and congregations of various denominations. In 1933, a group of black clergymen organized the National Fraternal Council of Negro Churches, an ecumenical structure designed (like the Federal Council of Churches) to promote cooperative action among member denominations in social as well as religious causes. During the 1940s and 1950s the Fraternal Council vigorously protested racial discrimination and, by means of its Washington bureau, lobbied Congress for the passage of civil rights legislation.[8]

Interdenominational cooperation did not disguise the serious doctrinal divisions that separated black Baptists from black Methodists and black Pentecostals. But despite their doctrinal differences, black Christians shared more with each other than they did with white Christians of the same denominations. The racial segregation of American churches stood as a continual reminder that Christianity had failed to build a biracial religious community in this country. None were more zealous in exposing this failure than were various groups of black Muslims and black Jews. Since the days of slavery, African-Americans had identified themselves metaphorically with biblical Israel in prayer, sermon, and song. The first organization to take this identification literally was the Church of God and Saints of Christ, founded in 1896 by William S. Crowdy in Lawrence, Kansas. Crowdy preached a heterodox version of Judaism based upon his assertion that black people were descended from the ten lost tribes of Israel. Similar beliefs inspired the development of other black Jewish congregations. In the 1920s, Wentworth A. Matthew formed around a nucleus of West Indian immigrants the Commandment Keepers Congregation of the Living God, for years Harlem's largest congregation of black Jews. The Commandment Keepers believed that African-Americans were "Ethiopian Hebrews" or Falashas, who had been stripped of their true religion by slavery. Judaism was the ancestral heritage of the Ethiopians, whereas Christianity was the religion of the "Gentiles," that is, whites. The Commandment Keepers rejected Christianity as the religion of a corrupt white society that would destroy itself in atomic warfare. They condemned emotionally expressive worship, so characteristic of black shouting-churches, as "niggerition." Moral restraint and dignity presumably distinguished the behavior of the Ethiopian Hebrew from the immorality and self-indulgence of the "typical" Negro. While they rejected racist stereotypes as applicable to themselves, black Jews accepted them as accurate descriptions of black behavior and black culture.[9]

Black Muslim groups closely resembled black Jews in the rejection of Negro identity as pejoratively defined by whites, and in the invention of a new religious-racial identity for African-Americans. The original religion of black people, they claimed, was Islam. The first organized movement of black Americans to identify itself as Muslim was the Moorish Science Temple founded in Newark, New Jersey, in 1913 by Timothy Drew. The

Noble Drew Ali, as his followers called him, taught that African-Americans were not Negroes but Asiatics. Their original home was Morocco; their true nationality was Moorish-American. To symbolize recovery of their true identity, members of the Moorish Science Temple received new names and identity cards issued by Noble Drew Ali. Knowledge of their true selves, Ali taught, would empower them to overcome racial oppression.[10] The Moorish Science Temple survived Ali's death in 1929, only to be eclipsed by another esoteric Muslim group that gained much more notoriety among blacks as well as whites.

In 1930 a peddler, W. D. Fard, began teaching poor blacks in Detroit that they were members of a Muslim "lost-found tribe of Shabbazz" and that salvation for black people lay in knowledge of self. Before disappearing in 1934, Fard provided an institutional base for his movement by establishing the Temple of Islam, the University (actually an elementary and secondary school) of Islam, the Muslim Girls Training Class, and a paramilitary corps, the Fruit of Islam. Under Fard's successor, Elijah Muhammad, who guided the movement for the next forty years, the Nation of Islam grew from two small congregations in Detroit and Chicago to dozens of mosques embracing thousands of members in every section of the country. By claiming that Fard had actually been the incarnation of Allah and that he was Fard-Allah's messenger, Elijah Muhammad asserted his authority to proclaim an elaborate gospel that owed much more to the racial situation in America than it did to the tenets of Islam. His revelation that white people were a race of devils, the product of a black scientist's malicious genetic experiment, was heresy in the eyes of orthodox Muslims, but to Messenger Elijah's disciples it seemed a plausible explanation for endemic white racism and an effective antidote to the pervasive myth of black inferiority.

The black Muslims, most notably Malcolm X, castigated black Christians for accepting the "white man's religion" and denounced the black church for keeping black Americans ignorant of their true selves. They pointed to their successful record in rehabilitating criminals, drug addicts, and alcoholics as proof that Islam was better fitted than Christianity to save the outcasts of America's society. Black Muslims, like black Jews, rejected behavior associated with popular black culture and disciplined their membership to observe strict dietary and social regulations. Moreover, black Muslims insisted on a new national as well as religious identity. Elijah Muhammad taught his followers to reject the rituals of American civic piety, such as saluting the flag, voting, and registering for the draft. Claiming that they constituted a black nation, the black Muslims demanded that the federal government set aside a separate section of the country for black people in compensation for the unpaid labor of their slave ancestors.[11]

Black Jewish and black Muslim attacks on Christianity highlighted a problem that had long troubled black churches: the racist attitudes and behavior of white Christians. From slavery days on, black Christians had resisted the temptation to identify Christianity as a religion "for whites only" by distinguishing "true" Christianity, which preached the equality of all races, from "false" Christianity, which countenanced slavery and discrimination against blacks. There were always those, however, who failed to see the distinction and who scorned Christianity as the religion of the oppressors. Given the history of white brutality against blacks, how could blacks accept the same religion as whites? The national identity of black Americans was threatened by the same dilemma. A history of slavery, disfranchisement, and discrimination in America made African-Americans feel like aliens in their own land. Black Jews and black Muslims solved the dilemma by embracing their alienation from Christianity and from America. By identifying with Judaism and Islam, respected religions embraced by millions of "nonwhite" people around the world, African-Americans figuratively escaped to a religious homeland outside the racial boundaries that imprisoned them in America. For some, the migration became actual. The Original Hebrew Israelites, for example, a black Jewish group from Chicago, emigrated in 1967 to Liberia and in 1969 to Israel, where their claims to original ownership of the land created problems for Israeli authorities.[12]

African-Americans also converted to orthodox forms of Islam and Judaism in twentieth-century America. As more black Americans were exposed to the interracial character of worldwide Judaism and Islam, the racialist doctrines of Crowdy, Ali, and Fard seemed false or at least outmoded. After the death of Elijah Muhammad in 1975, his son Warrithuddin (Wallace Deen) Muhammad began teaching that his father's doctrines were to be understood allegorically, not literally. He encouraged civic and political participation among black Muslims and even opened membership to whites. As the Nation of Islam moved rapidly toward orthodox Islam, it signified the shift by changing its name in 1976 to the World Community of Islam in the West, and in 1980, to the American Muslim Mission. These changes were rejected by some black Muslims, however, who remained loyal to the original teachings of Elijah Muhammad. Under the leadership of Minister Louis Farrakhan, they resumed the separatist ideals of the Nation of Islam.[13]

Faced with the discrepancy between the creed that American Christians preached and the deeds they performed, black Muslims rejected both America and Christianity, although doing so required them to deny significant aspects of their own history as African-Americans. For most black Americans, this was too high a price to pay. Instead, like generations before them, they refused to believe that America was a white man's country or that Christianity was a white man's religion. With increasing militancy, they continued to call upon the nation to "rise up and live out the true meaning of its creed," as Martin Luther King, Jr., put it in his keynote address at the 1963 March on Washington. And they used the symbols and the rhetoric of the black religious tradition to do so.

In 1966 the cry "black power" could be heard, signifying that some black activists were disappointed with the slow pace of racial change and disillusioned with the tactics of nonviolence. Black power quickly became a rallying cry for those who adopted a more radical position than King's. While King rejected the demand for black power as a slogan without a program, in 1966 the National Committee of Negro Churchmen (later renamed the National Conference of Black Churchmen) distanced itself from King by issuing an extended theological defense in the July 31 issue of the *New York Times*. The assassination of King in 1968 led to massive rioting in urban areas around the country and seemed to confirm that the period of nonviolent protest had passed. Self-determination, community control, and liberation replaced desegregation and integration as the catchwords of the movement. Radical militants joined the black Muslims in attacking the black church for being otherworldly, compensatory, and reactionary. Assertions of black pride and celebrations of black cultural identity marked a new mood of independence among black Americans. Separatism was on the rise while integration seemed discredited even in ecumenical circles.

In 1967, for example, black delegates to a National Council of Churches conference on urban problems insisted on splitting the meeting into two caucuses, one black and one white. Black Christians in white churches established ongoing caucuses to deal with issues of black identity and black autonomy. Between 1968 and 1970, black Catholics organized the Black Catholic Clergy Caucus, the National Black Sisters Conference, the Black Catholic Lay Caucus, and finally the National Office of Black Catholics, which proceeded to characterize the Catholic Church in America as primarily a white racist institution. In 1969 tensions between black clergy and white churches were exacerbated further when the civil rights activist James Forman presented a "Black Manifesto" demanding that white Christian churches and Jewish synagogues pay out $500 million for black economic development in reparation for slavery and racial oppression. Support for the manifesto by the National Conference of Black Churchmen led to bitter controversy between black clergy and white denominational boards over how much money should be given and to whom.[14]

In this context of militancy, separatism, and heated rhetoric, black churchmen began developing a black theology to articulate systematically the distinctive character of African-American religious experience. The most prolific and prominent of the black theologians was James H. Cone, professor at Union Theological Seminary in New York, whose first book, *Black Theology and Black Power*, appeared in 1969. As the title suggests, Cone's book was in part a response to the challenge presented to black Christians by the black power movement. What did Christianity have to do with the liberation and empowerment of black people? Cone's answer, further elaborated in successive books, was that God identifies himself in human history with the struggle of black people and has evidenced their ultimate victory in the resurrection of Jesus, who came to liberate the oppressed. Cone's black theology also leveled a strong attack against white theologians for failing even to consider the experience of the oppressed, which, he claimed, is the primary focus of God's saving presence in the world. Whereas Cone made liberation the major theme of his theology, other black theologians, like J. Deotis Roberts, emphasized reconciliation, or like historian of religion Charles Long, stressed the non-Christian components of black folk religion. During the past fifteen years, black American theologians have entered into discussion with African, Asian, feminist, and liberation theologians and have begun to add the issue of class to their theological reflections.[15]

Even before King's assassination, for reasons too numerous to summarize here, the civil rights movement had lost momentum, but his death, more clearly than anything else, marked the end of an identifiable movement for racial equality on the national level. No black leader of national stature arose to take his place, although the Reverend Jesse Jackson attempted to revive the spirit of the movement in his 1984 and 1988 political campaigns for the Democratic party's presidential nomination. Significantly, black churches played a strategic role in the local organization of his campaign nationwide. The absence of a national black political movement has distracted observers from considering the activity of black churches on the local level, where issues of community organization, housing, education, economic development, and employment have troubled black Americans for the past fifty years and more. A highly successful and widely imitated model of church-sponsored black economic development on the local level was the Opportunities Industrialization Center (OIC) founded in 1964 by Leon H. Sullivan, author of the "Sullivan Principles" and pastor of Zion Baptist Church in Philadelphia. The OIC trained unemployed and underemployed black and white workers for skilled positions in industry and assisted them in finding jobs to match their newly acquired skills. By the end of the decade, similar OIC programs were established across the country. OIC was preceded by a "selective patronage campaign" in which, on a given Sunday, four hundred black ministers urged their congregations not to patronize a particular company because it discriminated against blacks in employment. An estimated twenty-nine selective patronage campaigns between 1959 and 1963 opened up many jobs formerly closed to blacks in Philadelphia and inspired the Southern Christian Leadership Conference to establish a similar program, Operation Breadbasket, in 1962. In numerous black communities, black churches have sponsored housing improvement and neighborhood development programs, health care clinics, day-care centers, and senior citizen facilities.[16]

For most of the past fifty years, scholars have asserted that secular alternatives were diminishing the extent of the black church's power in the black community—a difficult assertion to verify. Evidence is conflicting, and what type of evidence to use is unclear. Recently, for example, social analysts have listed the waning influence of religious values upon inner-city blacks as a contributing factor to the current crises of teenage pregnancies, illegitimate births, absent-father households, drug abuse, and "black on black" crime. Yet the same social planners looked to the black church as the primary community agency to deal with these intractable problems of America's black underclass. Certainly black Americans, like whites, have been exposed to modern secular culture. But, statistically at least, the black church has remained strong. In 1936 the United States Census for Religious Bodies estimated that there were 5.7 million church members in a black population of 12.8 million. According to the 1986 edition of the *Yearbook of American and Canadian Churches*, black Baptists numbered more than 9 million, black Methodists roughly 4 million, and the black Holiness-Pentecostal family probably exceeded 4 million members. While these figures, based on church reports, were surely inflated, there is no reason to doubt that a large percentage of the approximately 28 million black Americans are church members. Yet the efficacy of social programs and the size of membership rolls are not the only, nor necessarily the most revealing measures of the black church's significance over the past five decades. The centrality of the church in the black American's quest for identity and meaning has demonstrated its ongoing resilience and creativity during a period of tumultuous change.

Chapter Six

Minority within a Minority: The History of Black Catholics in America

IF ASKED TO DESCRIBE THE RELIGION of black Americans, most people would think of large black Baptist, Methodist, and Holiness-Pentecostal denominations as the historic centers of African-American religious life in this country. They would also identify the religion of African-Americans with the spirituals, gospel music, chanted sermons, and emotionally expressive forms of worship—the staples of Evangelical Protestant piety. Similarly, if asked to describe Roman Catholicism in America, most people would probably remark on the immigrant background of American Catholics, identifying the Irish, Germans, Italians, Poles, and Hispanics as the distinctive ethnic groups within the church. Black Catholics, if they come to mind at all, are thought of as somewhat anomalous, since they represent such a small percentage of the black population in the United States. Indeed, they are a minority within a minority: Catholic blacks are a minority within the African-American population, itself a minority. There are approximately 1.2 million black Catholics in the United States. Four of every 100 black Americans are Roman Catholics. And black Catholics are a minority within the American Catholic population, also a minority. Two out of every 100 American Catholics are black. As we shall see, this "minority within a minority status" has had profound implications for the religious and racial identities of black Catholics in the United States.

Of course, considered in hemispheric perspective, a large number of African-Americans are Catholic. It was the settled policy of Portugal that all slaves brought into her New World colony of Brazil had to be baptized before the slave ships set sail from Africa. Similarly, the slave codes of the French and Spanish colonies legislated that slaveowners baptize and instruct their slaves in the Catholic faith. Though instruction was minimal, Haitian, Cuban, and Brazilian slaves did, as we've seen, meld certain aspects of Catholicism with African religions to form Voodoo, Santería, and Candomblé.

At any rate, blacks have been part of the Catholic Church since its beginnings in America. John Carroll, the first American bishop, noted in 1785 in his report to Rome on the state of Catholicism in America that 3,000 of the 15,800 Catholics in Maryland were black slaves owned by Catholic masters, including the Jesuits, who held slaves to work their estates. Carroll complained that American Catholics, like their Protestant countrymen, had done little to instruct their slaves in the doctrines and rules of the faith. In far-off Louisiana, Carroll reported, there were settlements of French Catholics.[1] There the Capuchin friars had taken on the mission to convert the slaves as early as 1722. But outside the settlement of New Orleans, the bulk of the slave population was widely scattered on distant plantations, separated by miles of wilderness, accessible only by boat. Although French and Spanish priests did baptize large groups of slaves twice a year, on Holy Saturday and on the Vigil of Pentecost, and colonial baptismal registers in Louisiana teem with entries for slaves and free blacks, baptism was rarely succeeded by instruction. Few Louisiana slaves received the regular pastoral care or the sacraments of this widely scattered mission church.

Outside Louisiana and Maryland, small pockets of black Catholics could be found, for example, in the area of Bardstown, Kentucky, where Catholics from Maryland settled with their slaves at the beginning of the nineteenth century. A few more black Catholics were located in St. Louis and other trading outposts of the French in the Mississippi valley. The overwhelming majority of blacks were slaves in the Protestant South and had little or no contact with Catholicism. And sometimes those who did, didn't like what they saw. "We was all supposed to be Catholics on our place, but lots didn't like that 'ligion," recalled Elizabeth Ross Hite, who belonged to a Catholic master. "We used to hide behind some bricks and hold church ourselves. You see, the Catholic preachers from France wouldn't let us shout, and the Law done said you gotta shout if you want to be saved. That's in the Bible." An elderly slave from Virginia who had been sold to Louisiana forty years earlier remarked on the differences between Protestant and Catholic piety when he confessed to the traveler Frederick Law Olmsted, "Oh Sar, they don't have no meetin' o' no kind round here."[2] Prayer meetings, shouting, and spirituals—the touchstones of black Evangelicalism—were foreign to the experience of black Catholics. Nevertheless, there were slaves and free blacks who were attracted to the centuries-old rituals of Catholicism. They found deep meaning in the Mass, the sacraments, and in personal devotion to the Virgin and the Saints. The experience of Pierre Landry, a slave in Louisiana, illustrates the power of the Catholic liturgical tradition to speak to blacks as well as whites.

My early religious training was in the Roman Catholic Church at Donaldsonville. I was prepared for first communion in a large class of both white and colored youths. The sacrament was administered on an Easter Sunday morning, and I shall never forget the impressiveness of the services that day. The august presence of the bishop who confirmed the class was to me typical of extraordinary grandeur and power, and when it came to my turn to kiss the signet ring of His Grace, the jewel appeared to me as a blazing torch in which were reflected the burning candles of the resplendent altar.³ (Nevertheless, after Emancipation, Landry became a Methodist minister.)

It was primarily in the cities of Baltimore and New Orleans that sizable countries of black Catholics emerged, centered around "free persons of color," former slaves of racially mixed ancestry, who had been freed and in some cases educated. In New Orleans this French-speaking, proudly self-aware group of "colored Creoles" was augmented by refugees from the revolution in Haiti of 1791. Significant numbers of Haitian émigrés, some slave, but most free, also settled in Baltimore (and in smaller numbers in New York, Philadelphia, and Charleston). The basement chapel of St. Mary's Seminary served as their parish church. There Sulpician priests who had fled the revolution in France ministered to the religious needs of the émigrés and their children. In New Orleans, nineteenth-century visitors to the city frequently noted with surprise the presence of "colored" Catholics in St. Louis Cathedral and other churches of the city. The free people of color formed a caste apart, between whites and blacks. In some instances, they inherited or amassed enough property to become slaveowners themselves. In both New Orleans and Baltimore, this distinctive group formed the core of the black Catholic community for much of the nineteenth century.

In these cities two communities of black nuns originated, the Oblate Sisters of Providence founded in Baltimore in 1829 and the Holy Family Sisters in New Orleans in 1842. The Oblate Sisters emerged out of the Haitian refugee community that congregated for worship in the basement of the seminary. Of the four young women who founded the community, Marie Balas and Rosine Boegues were Haitian, Elizabeth Lange was from Cuba, and Theresa Duchemin, though American-born, was of French-speaking parents. Parenthetically, Duchemin later left the Oblates and in 1845 formed a community of sisters in Michigan, the Sister Servants of the Immaculate Heart of Mary. These women, under the direction of Father James Joubert, a French Sulpician, formed themselves into a religious community in order to teach black children to read, so that they could then take catechism classes in preparation for confirmation and their first communion. On June 2, 1829, the sisters took their first promises and in 1831 their community was officially approved by Pope Gregory XVI. Despite the prejudice of white Catholics—"who," according to Joubert, "could not accept the idea of these poor girls (colored girls) wearing the habit of [the] religious"—despite nagging poverty, despite the suggestion of Bishop Eccleston of Baltimore that they disband, this small community of black women survived, slowly increased in number, and continued to teach black children in the antebellum South.[4]

A decade after the foundation of the Oblate Sisters, a white French woman, Josephine Alicot, who had been instructing slaves on Louisiana plantations, encouraged three free women of color, Harriet Delisle and Josephine Charles of New Orleans and Juliette Gaudin, a Haitian refugee, to consecrate themselves to God. With the approval of their bishop, they opened a house on St. Bernard Street in November 1842, the first house of the Sisters of the Holy Family. They taught catechism to young and old women to prepare them for Holy Communion, and eventually extended their ministry to staff an asylum for aged and infirm women, an academy for girls, and several day schools.

The existence of these black sisterhoods illustrates the extent of segregation in nineteenth-century Catholic religious communities. Without the Oblates and the Holy Family Sisters, black Catholic women had no access to the religious life. An experimental interracial convent of the Sisters of Loretto in Kentucky had ended in failure because the time was not auspicious for such a venture, according to one priest. Started by Father Charles Nerinckx, an early missionary to Kentucky Catholics, the experiment was marred by discrimination from the outset. Nerinckx declared of the black sisters: "Their dress is to be different, also their offices and employment, but they keep the main rules of the society—they will take the vows, but not the perpetual ones before twelve years of profession."[5] The first five novices lived apart from the other sisters. After Nerinckx left Kentucky for Missouri, his successor, Father Guy Chasbrot, released the black sisters from their obligations and sent them back to their homes.

The Oblate Sisters of Providence and the Holy Family Sisters gave black women the opportunity, otherwise denied to them, to heed their vocation to the religious life. These black nuns made a practical contribution to their communities by educating black children when no one else in the church would. They also made an extremely important symbolic contribution to the faith of black Catholics by giving them the chance to see some of their own living the vowed life of the religious. The black nuns were all the more important since the crucial avenue to religious authority, the priesthood, remained virtually closed to black Catholics during the nineteenth century. While a black Baptist and a Methodist clergy had emerged late in the eighteenth century, it took another century for black Catholic priests to begin pastoring their own people. The Catholic view of the priest as a sacral figure, ordained primarily to officiate at the holy sacrifice of the Mass, differed significantly from the Protestant notion of the minister as preacher of the Word. The sacral character and the necessity of meticulous training in liturgical gesture and language made it impossible for a Catholic layman to assume the role of priest, in contrast to the relative ease with which a Baptist, for example, could become a preacher. As a result, the status and the authority of the black Protestant minister were not duplicated among black Catholics.

The first black Americans ordained to the priesthood were

James, Patrick, and Alexander Sherwood Healy, the sons of a mulatto slave mother, Mary Elisa, and an Irish immigrant father, Michael Morris Healy. Born in Georgia, all three were sent North to be educated, first at a Quaker school on Long Island and then at the newly formed College of the Holy Cross in Worcester, Massachusetts. All three did their seminary training and were ordained to the priesthood in Europe in the mid nineteenth century. Cosmopolitan, highly educated, urbane, and talented men, the Healys returned from Europe to face prejudice in their own land and in their own church. Patrick Healy, while acting dean of students at Holy Cross, wrote to Father George Fenwick, his spiritual director, in 1853: "Father, I will be candid with you. Placed in a college as I am, over boys who were well acquainted with me or my brothers, remarks are sometimes made (though not in my hearing) which wound my very heart. You know to what I refer." And when Alexander Sherwood Healy was named as a potential candidate for rectorship of the North American College in Rome, Bishop Fitzpatrick of Boston wrote Archbishop Hughes of New York explaining why Healy wouldn't do: "It would be useless to recommend him even were he known to other bishops as well as to myself. His youth would be a fatal objection. There is also another objection which, though in reason less substantial, would in fact be quite as stubborn. He has African blood and it shows distinctly in his exterior. This, in a large number of American youths, might lessen the respect they ought to feel for the first superior in a house."[6] Prejudice aside, the Healys rose to significant positions of authority in the American Catholic Church. James became chancellor of the archdiocese of Boston and then bishop of Portland, Maine, Alexander taught in Boston's diocesan seminary, and Patrick, a Jesuit, became president of Georgetown University.

Though it was generally known that the light-skinned Healys had African ancestry, they were not publicly acclaimed as black priests, as was Augustus Tolton. Born a slave in Missouri, Tolton,

like the Healys, had to go abroad to seek seminary training. As a
matter of fact, on the eve of his ordination in Rome in 1886, Tolton
was still uncertain whether he would be sent back to America,
since there was some question in the minds of his Roman superiors
about his impact as the only black priest in the United States. Returning home, he founded a parish for black Catholics in Chicago.
The publicity that greeted Tolton's return and the popularity of
his ministry indicated the pride of black Americans (Protestant as
well as Catholic) that one of their number had been elevated to the
priesthood. It also revealed the novelty of the idea of a black clergy
in the American Catholic Church. Some Catholics felt that blacks
were not yet worthy of the dignity of the priesthood, lamenting
what they delicately called a "lack of the tradition of celibacy
among blacks." A vocal minority argued, as did Father John R.
Slattery of the Josephites, that black Catholics should have their
own priests. Slattery went on to blame the scarcity of black priests
upon the prejudice of Irish-American clergy. Preaching the ordination Mass of a black priest, Father John Henry Dorsey in
1902, Slattery did not mince his words:

> As far as her fundamental system goes, the Catholic Church rec-
> ognizes no race. . . . Perhaps it is the wisest policy to admit frankly
> that because a man enters the Sanctuary or a woman the Cloister
> he or she is still human and carries along the passions and preju-
> dices of his or her part of the country. No matter what Catholicism
> ought to do and may have done in the past, the fact is as clear as
> the noonday Sun that many Catholics to-day are prejudiced against
> the Negro. It is this uncatholic sentiment which looks askance on
> Negro priests. Now the common objection to Negro priests is on
> the score of morality. We do not think the Whites can afford to
> throw stones at the Blacks on this point. Mulattoes, quadroons,
> and such folks drop not from the skies. For ages concubinage was
> rife among the clergy of Europe.[7]

It did not help matters when Slattery published the sermon. The
chancellor of the diocese attacked Slattery in print, and Slattery

rebutted his attack in print. Nor did it help the cause when Slattery, the foremost spokesman for the ordination of black men to the priesthood, himself left the priesthood, abandoned Catholicism, got married, and started attacking celibacy and Catholic doctrine in print.

In 1891, Tolton was followed by Charles Randolph Uncles, a Josephite, as the next black American ordained to the priesthood and the first ordained in the United States. After Uncles, John Henry Dorsey and John J. Plantevigne were ordained as Josephites after the turn of the century. The first black diocesan priest to be accepted and trained in a seminary in the United States was Stephen Theobald, ordained by Archbishop John Ireland in St. Paul, Minnesota, in 1910. Finally, in 1920 a major breakthrough in the development of a black Catholic clergy occurred when the Society of the Divine Word opened St. Augustine's Seminary in Bay St. Louis, Mississippi, specifically to train black youth for the priesthood, since they were still unwelcome in the seminaries for most dioceses and religious orders.

These pioneer black priests faced heartbreaking obstacles. Committed, well-trained, idealistic, they frequently faced unexpected prejudice, misunderstanding, and humiliation within the very church to which they had dedicated their lives. The case of John Plantevigne, while extreme, is illustrative of the kinds of scandal that black priests had to tolerate. Born in rural Louisiana, Plantevigne had attended Straight University in New Orleans but left Straight in order to enter the Josephites in Baltimore. Ordained in 1907, he was assigned to preach parish missions in the South. Having completed several tours successfully, Plantevigne was stunned when Archbishop James Blenk refused to allow him to preach in New Orleans. Plantevigne's letter to Blenk poignantly reveals his pain:

> Rev. and dear Archbishop Blenk,
> I just returned from Mobile, Alabama, last night where father

Albert and I gave a three week mission and a most successful one. On arriving here in Mississippi, I found the most distressful news awaiting me and that was your refusal to accept me into your city to conduct a mission there. Death would have been more welcome to me than such news. So far I have been giving missions with father Albert in the dioceses of Wilmington, Del., Baltimore, Md., Richmond, Va., Mobile, Ala., and have met no objection from . . . bishops, priests, nor laymen white or colored. All the missions we gave were considered a Godsend by all the colored people and also the priests in whose churches we gave them because the fact of my being colored did away with the prejudice the non-Catholics had against the church and caused many to come into the fold of Christ. The white people had no objection and attended the missions even in Mobile night after night, and among them were doctors, lawyers, as well as the ordinary people. Not only did they attend the mission but came to the house to see me and wish me success.

Now dear bishop, to be refused the privilege of giving the mission in New Orleans by you, my own bishop, has cast the deepest gloom over me. When I left Straight University to go to Baltimore to study for the priesthood those who were against the Catholic Church predicted just such obstacles. I defended my church, and going through the greatest hardship, I became a priest to find these predictions coming true and from [my] own diocese. I feel almost despondent.

However, I have not yet given up but hope that your objections may arise from the fact that you do not know how successful I have been and with what cordiality I have been received by all. Surely New Orleans, a city wherein there are so many Catholics ought not to be the exception.

The news of your refusal to receive me as a missionary will fly through the country and do untold harm to the cause of the Catholic Church among my people. The enemies of the church who are working among the colored people are continually holding up these things before them and this will be looked upon as a proof of all they have said whether true or false.

Give me at least a trial. "No man should be condemned without a trial." Then, if I fail to give satisfaction our enemies cannot blame the church. I have written to all my friends saying I was coming to New Orleans to give the mission and hoped thereby to give the lie to . . . the Church's enemies. Now your refusal will hinder our cause and cause a still greater leak among my people. Please let me hear from you and do not let me continue in this agony of spirit.   Yours in Christ,

                                                                               J. J. Plantevigne[8]

Archbishop Blenk's response was blunt: the time was not right. He would act prudently and carefully in the cause of colored Catholics, not wanting to stir up contention. Plantevigne wrote again, and his concluding words echo the disillusionment that would affect the rest of his life: "My life has been made most miserable and my course changed altogether by your stand. All the good I have been doing by giving these missions and dispelling the prejudice of my own people who have been made to realize so often the bitterness of many against them in mixt congregations shall be put to naught. I myself in spite of what you say feel like a castaway and my life is miserable."[9]

Plantevigne's disillusionment was no doubt deepened by his own personal history. His brother Albert had abandoned Catholicism at Straight University and had become a teacher and a Congregationalist minister back in Point Coupee, Louisiana. He had persisted in starting a school for black children in spite of white opposition. He was found on a dusty road one day, with his head bashed in. Father Plantevigne, according to Albert Foley, who sketched his life in a pioneering book on black Catholic priests, *God's Men of Color*, never forgot the refusal of his bishop to allow him to preach. Two years later the *Afro-American Ledger* reported Plantevigne's remarks to a conference of missionaries held in Washington, D. C.:

The blood of the Negro boils in resentment of a "Jim-Crow" system in the Catholic Church. The doors of the Church must be opened full width, not a side entrance, if the Negro is to be saved by the Catholic Church. Negroes have followed their masters into the Catholic Church, but have fallen away in great numbers because they have not been given an active part in the organic life of the Church. Social circumstances compel us to compromise. This is unfortunate because it loses the Negro and fails to develop true religion among the whites, for true religion is charity. The Negro wants Catholic priests; non-Catholic people are accustomed to colored ministers and refuse to enter the Catholic Church under white priests.[10]

Eventually, Plantevigne had a nervous and physical breakdown. Hospitalized, he died of tuberculosis at forty-two years of age. Plantevigne's case and the defection of Slattery reinforced the opinion among the hierarchy that ordaining black men was a risky and imprudent business. As Plantevigne, Slattery, and others realized, the failure of the American Catholic Church to develop an African-American clergy until the mid twentieth century was a crucial factor in the slow growth of Catholicism among black Americans. The scarcity of black priests made black Catholics seem like wards of a white-controlled institution.

The absence of a black Catholic clergy did not prevent black laity from asserting that the true religious home of black people was Roman Catholicism. From 1889 to 1894, delegates from different sections of the country met together in five annual congresses of African-American Catholics. They met to discuss common issues, to encourage education of black Catholic youth, and to protest discrimination within the church. The organizer and leading spirit of these congresses was Daniel A. Rudd, a descendant of Catholic slaves from Kentucky. Rudd, a journalist by profession, edited and published a black Catholic newspaper, the *American Catholic Tribune*. In the pages of the *Tribune*, Rudd conducted a running battle with black Protestant editors, such as the

Episcopalian George Bragg and the Baptist William Simmons. He argued that salvation for African-Americans, personally and racially, lay not in Protestant "race churches" but in the universalism of Catholicism.

A revealing paradox emerges from the pages of the *Tribune* and the proceedings of the congresses: Rudd and his colleagues argued that the "Catholic Church alone [could] break the color line." Addressing Protestant blacks, who were welcomed at the congresses as honored guests, they contended that the Church Universal transcended the divisive particularities of nationality and race. Yet the congresses were compelled to protest vigorously against discrimination from white Catholics. Thus, on the one hand, they held up the image of the age-old Church of Rome, which had, as Robert L. Ruffin of Boston remarked to the third congress in Philadelphia,

> in her early history among her communicants . . . not only blacks but persons of both sexes holding most exalted positions. There were holy women like St. Monica, St. Felicita, and St. Perpetua. There were holy men like St. Augustine, St. Basil, St. Cyprian, St. Moses, St. Benedict the Moor, St. Cyril, all of whom, as the Church affirms, were of pure Ethiopian blood, and the Church has always represented that one among the wise men who came to present the newborn Saviour with costly gifts was a Negro.[11]

On the other hand, the same congress challenged the exclusion of black children over twelve years of age from Catholic schools. The delegates appointed a committee to gather reports of discrimination, circulate questionnaires among American bishops on the matter, and report their findings to the Pope in Rome. The fifth congress turned out to be the last. Cardinal Gibbons and his advisors thought it best that these lay congresses cease.

The activism of Rudd and his colleagues in the African-

American Catholic congresses was taken up in the twentieth century by the Federated Colored Catholics, founded in 1917 by
Thomas Wyatt Turner, a descendant of Catholic slaves from
southern Maryland and a professor of biology first at Howard University and then at Hampton Institute. Turner, like Rudd before
him, combined a deep commitment to Catholicism with a dedication to active protest for racial justice. The Federated Colored
Catholics organized black Catholics nationally, developed black
leadership locally, and protested discrimination within and without the church. A major target of the federation was segregation
in Catholic educational institutions such as the Catholic University of America and St. Louis University, whose doors were closed
to black students until the 1940s. Initially, Turner enjoyed the
friendship and cooperation of two white Jesuits, Father William
Markoe and Father John La Farge, pioneers in the apostolate of
interracial justice. But as Marilyn Wentzke Nickels demonstrates,
Turner split with the two priests over the basic purpose and direction of the organization he had founded. He saw it primarily as
an organization of black Catholics united to achieve equality
within the church; the two priests saw it as a forum for interracial
cooperation and rejected the black identity of the group as reverse
racism. When Father Markoe engineered a change in the name of
the federation's journal, from the *Chronicle of the Federated Colored
Catholics* to the *Interracialist*, a change symbolic of the shift in
overall direction toward interracialism, the organization split in
two. Turner's faction, diminished in numbers and influence,
lasted until the mid-1950s. Turner and the federation refused to
allow discrimination to drive them from the church. Instead they
expressed a new mood of militancy in claiming the church as their
own:

> The Catholic colored people have tied themselves in the Church
> ... to the Banner of the Lord Jesus Christ, which we think we
> recognize quite clearly; but when a whiter majority in the Church

shall for social purposes abandon this Banner we shall certainly not be misled. If all the White priests and laymen decide that segregation and discriminating Catholics are reasonable in the Catholic Church we shall still cling to the undefiled Banner of the Lord even though we may have to "tread the winepress alone."[12]

Though the Federated Colored Catholics were visible proof that not all blacks were Protestant, until the mid twentieth century there were scarcely enough black Catholics, except in Maryland and Louisiana, to notice. In 1890, a generous estimate of the number of black Catholics in the United States was 200,000. At that date most blacks still lived in the rural South, where Catholics were few and far between. Without a special mission to convert them, most blacks had no direct contact with Catholicism. Shortly after the Civil War, the American bishops, gathered at the Second Plenary Council of Baltimore (1866), took up the question (at the insistence of Rome) of the spiritual condition of the freedmen. Several suggested the establishment of a vicar apostolic, a man of episcopal rank, to oversee and coordinate missions to the former slaves. Others rejected the plan as unnecessary and unworkable. (Several southern bishops made fun of the idea.) The council failed to come up with a practical plan and left action up to the discretion, and the resources, of individual bishops.

As the church in America faced new waves of Catholic immigration from southern and eastern Europe from 1870 to 1914, even those bishops who wanted to had few resources available to establish a large-scale mission to blacks, though some urged them to do just that. Appeals to American and European religious orders for priests and nuns to labor in this field gained some response, but not nearly enough given the immensity of the task. From England came the Mill Hill Fathers, who developed an American branch called the Josephites, the first society of men to take up the mission to African-Americans as their special vocation. Herbert, later Cardinal Vaughan, the founder of the Mill Hill

Fathers, toured America in 1871 to survey his society's new mission field. He quickly marked the racial attitudes with which the missionaries would need to cope:

> I can give you no idea of the dislike of the Americans, Southerners as well as Northerners to the Negroes. It far exceeds in intensity and subtlety anything I had expected. How can any race deserve to be blessed by God when they refuse to recognize as brethren those who have the same Father in Heaven, and the same Redeemer on earth? I assure you it makes my blood run cold. And I am in a state of chronic irritation. Priests and Religious look upon us with the same kind of wonder that we should entertain for an Order of men who have made a vow to live in the wards of a smallpox hospital. Poor Negro-race, has it come to this? Or rather, should I say, poor Christians, is this your state?[13]

The Josephites worked exclusively among black people and, as we've already seen, proved willing to accept black men into their society and to train them for the priesthood. In addition to the Josephites, the Holy Ghost Fathers, beginning in 1891, and the Society of the Divine Word, in 1906, sent men to work in the racially troubled world of the American South. In 1891, a new order of nuns, the Sisters of the Blessed Sacrament, was founded by Katherine Drexel to educate African-Americans and Native Americans. Heir to the Drexel fortune, Mother Katherine supported innumerable missions, churches, and schools throughout the South and Southwest. In 1915, she laid the foundation for Xavier University to provide black Catholics with an institution of higher education. Over the years, the white priests and nuns of these and other religious communities made major contributions to the growth of Catholicism among black Americans, in the midst of difficulties that Vaughan only glimpsed.

Gradually, in the late nineteenth century, separate black Catholic churches became the norm rather than the exception as more and more bishops decided to place blacks in ethnically derived instead of geographically determined parishes. The black Catholic population began to move from its traditional centers in Louisiana and Maryland to other areas as well. As rural blacks migrated to cities and from the South to the North and the West in steadily increasing numbers after the turn of the century, they came into contact with Catholics. Initially, the contact was none too friendly, as ethnic fears and economic rivalry roused racial animosity between the black migrants and Catholics of Irish, German, Italian, and Polish backgrounds. As they arrived, blacks replaced European immigrants in the urban ghettos or settled into blocks adjacent to them. For the first time, black Protestants met black Catholics who had migrated from Louisiana and the Gulf Coast. Usually, one or two Catholic churches remained in the changing neighborhoods to accomodate old parishioners and to convert newcomers. As time went on, the parochial school, which offered urban blacks an appealing alternative to public education, became an important source of black converts, exposed to the pervasive and mandatory Catholicism of the catechism and religion classes. As some social scientists have suggested, the desire for education and upward social mobility may have led some blacks to consider converting to Catholicism. However this may be, the number of black Catholics increased dramatically owing to conversion. Between 1940 and 1975, the black Catholic population grew from 296,988 to 916,854, an increase of 208 percent. From 2.3 percent, black Catholics grew to 4 percent of the black population.

These decades of growth for black Catholics also witnessed the development of the civil rights movement and the turbulent era of desegregation. The Catholic Church, no less than society at large, was divided in these tumultuous years. In 1947, Archbishop Joseph Ritter of St. Louis, Missouri, desegregated the Catholic schools of his archdiocese and did not hesitate to excommunicate Catholic segregationists who threatened court action against his decision. In the late 1950s and early 1960s, Archbishop Joseph

Rummel of New Orleans placed a rural parish under interdict (no observance of the sacraments) for refusing to allow a black priest to say Mass and excommunicated several prominent segregationists for resisting parochial school integration. While individual bishops were in the vanguard in desegregating schools, others were accused by their own priests of lagging behind in the pursuit of racial equality. When priests and nuns marched for open housing legislation, with Martin Luther King, Jr., and Father James Groppi, they were stoned and spat upon by the Catholic residents of east Chicago, and southside Milwaukee.

As black demands moved from integration to assertions of black separatism and black pride, black Catholics themselves experienced a crisis of identity. In the midst of celebrations of black pride and rediscoveries of black culture, some wondered where black Catholics fit? Were they not, after all, blacks in a white church, a church that still exhibited strains of racism? Had not African-American culture been overwhelmingly Protestant? What did Catholicism have to do with the spirituals or the ecstatic worship so characteriatic of black religion? Though the number of black priests has grown, were not most black Catholics still pastored by white priests? In order to address these and other questions, the Black Catholic Clergy Caucus, the National Black Sisters Conference, the Black Catholic Lay Caucus, and finally the National Office of Black Catholics were organized between 1968 and 1970. The Black Clergy Caucus criticized the Catholic Church in the United States as "primarily a white racist institution," which "has addressed itself primarily to white society," and urged the church to engage in institutional, attitudinal, and societal change.[14] Not content with criticism, the National Office of Black Catholics and local communities of black Catholics have sought over the past decade to define the meaning of Catholicism for themselves liturgically, theologically, and historically.

The process of self-definition has been difficult. Blacks, like other Catholics, do not automatically agree. Some have welcomed the introduction of black Protestant styles of worship to the traditional liturgy, already opened to change by Vatican II. Others have been less enthusiastic about changes in liturgy they have known for decades. Similarly, the quest for a black theology, led by black Protestant theologians, has not yet inspired a distinctive enterprise among black Catholic theologians, even though liberation theology has been strongly influenced by Latin American Catholics. Few black Catholics, however, have failed to welcome the reclamation of black Catholic history with interest and pride. In 1935, black Catholic bishops of the United States issued a pastoral letter, "What We Have Seen and Heard," calling for black Catholics to articulate the lessons of their peculiar history for the benefit of the Church Universal.

That history stretches back at least two centuries in the United States and is marked by a distinctive experience of religion and race: set apart from other Catholics by race and from other blacks by religion, black Catholics have a heightened sense of the "double consciousness" that, as W. E. B. Du Bois claimed, characterizes African-Americans generally. Catholic blacks, as a religious minority, have defended their religion to the black Protestant majority by asserting the universality of the church. Black Catholics, as a racial minority, have attacked discrimination and continually faced their own particularity as a people set apart. Religious universalism and racial particularism have been the two poles of black Catholic consciousness, rising out of their singular position as a minority within a minority.

Continuously, black Catholics have maintained that the church knows no race. Dan Rudd argued that blacks should convert to Catholicism because it erases the color line. The universalism of the church was construed as conclusive evidence for the truth claims of Catholicism. When confronted by contradictory evidence—acts of discrimination by fellow Catholics and Catholic institutions—black Catholics looked beyond America to the teachings and example of the Church Universal. While some white Catholics might be prejudiced, the Catholic Church extended around the world, embracing dark peoples in Africa and Asia. While blacks might be prohibited from some Catholic institutions, the church had placed blacks in positions of authority and canonized black saints in the past. While American seminaries might prohibit black candidates, the church was ordaining people of color in mission lands. While individual priests might be bigots, the sacraments worked *ex opere operato*, independent of the disposition of the priest. The Mass and popular devotions linked black Catholics to the timeless, cosmopolitan Church of Rome, which was one, holy, apostolic, and Catholic.

And yet, at the same time, black Catholics knew all too painfully that race did matter in the church in America. Though they might praise the church's universality in one breath, they actively protested discrimination with the next. The experience of black Catholics in the United States, then, has been an experience of alternating tension between the pull of universalism and the demands of racial particularism.

For the majority of black Protestants, this tension was solved long ago by forming separate black churches and denominations, an alternative not open to black Catholics. Black Baptists and African Methodists distanced themselves from the quandary by forming separate racial-religious institutions in which they controlled their own affairs, disciplined themselves, admitted and dismissed their own members, and called their own pastors. In a word they frequently used, black Methodists and Baptists functionally and institutionally exercised their "Christian manhood" rights.

Black Catholics might have done the same had they been willing, like the Polish National Catholic Church, for example, to go into schism, but this went against the very grain of their Catholic identity. They were thus caught within the structures of the institutional church. From within they proclaimed the universalism of the gospel. In so doing, they stood witness to a lesson both profound and simple. The Gospel and the Church are indeed universal. But they are, of necessity, universal in a particular way. That is, just as the historical Jesus became man in a particular time and place, among a particular people, so the universal Christ must become incarnate in all races, cultures, and times, for there is no leap to a spurious, colorless universalism. Unless we recognize cultural particularism, universalism becomes another word for the cultural hegemony of the dominant group. Black Catholic history reaffirms an old truth: the Church must never be confused with any particular ethnic group, race, culture, or period. The Church does indeed transcend race, but only by including all races within its embrace as equally valuable children, whose differences and unique contributions help to build up the Body of Christ. In this sense, black Catholic history has been an extended gloss on Galatians 3:28: "There is neither Jew nor Greek, there is neither slave nor free, there is neither male nor female; for you are all one in Christ Jesus."

Part III

The Performed Word

Religious Practice

Chapter Seven

The Chanted Sermon

Sunday after Sunday, for more than a century and a half, black ministers have moved their congregations to religious ecstacy by a distinctive style of preaching. Sometimes called the "black folk sermon" or "old-time country preaching," this complex verbal art is governed by strict performance rules that require skill and dedication to master. This kind of sermon is "old-time" in the sense that it is a traditional genre whose origins stretch back to the eighteenth century. But it is also a hardy perennial, alive and healthy in the modern day. It is "country" since its development took place primarily in the prayer meetings and revivals of the rural South. But it has long since spread West and North to the cities, where radio, television, and records extend the preachers' voices beyond the churches into the cars and homes of their flocks. This preaching style is a "folk" art because it is a creation of popular rather than elite culture and because it is an oral rather than literary form. However, the "folk" are notoriously difficult to define, and this tradition of preaching remains popular among literate and "sophisticated" congregations. Though "old-time" and "folk" are part of the aura surrounding this kind of preaching, the term "chanted" more accurately describes its defining characteristic, the metrical, tonal, rhythmic chant with which the preacher climaxes the sermon.[1]

The chanted sermon, while it is usually identified with black

141

preachers, is not an exclusively black tradition; neither is it inclusive of all the preaching styles used by black ministers. Some whites preach in this manner, and there have always been some black ministers who preach in an altogether different idiom. Nevertheless, the chanted sermon is as much a staple of African-American culture as spirituals, gospel, blues, and tales. Like these other forms of oral literature, the sermon has served as a source of information, advice, wisdom, and, not least, sheer enjoyment for generations of black Americans. This sermonic style has spread outside the pulpit to influence public speaking and singing styles in the secular sphere. Black and white literary artists as varied as Paul Laurence Dunbar, James Weldon Johnson, William Faulkner, Toni Morrison, Paule Marshalle, and Ralph Ellison have attempted to capture the cadences and esthetic effect of the chanted sermon.[2]

Because the oral rather than the written word has been the primary bearer of black culture, verbal skill is valued highly in the black community. As is the case with oral tradition in general, so here, too, the individual verbal artist earns critical recognition not by introducing something new, but by performing the old with skill, fluency, spontaneity, and intensity. Style of delivery determines the success of the oral performer whether bluesman, gospel singer, or preacher. It is not, then, merely the word as spoken — much less as read — but the word as *performed* that must be taken into account if the sermon is to be adequately understood. In this case, more than in most, style is content. For this reaon, the chanted sermon cannot be given full justice in print.[3]

The formal structure of the sermon derives from the Evangelical Protestant belief that the sermonic words should be devoted to explaining the Word. The presence of the Bible on the pulpit is a visual reminder of this close connection. It is customary for the preacher to begin by reading a text chosen from the Old or New

Testament, which is supposed to indicate the theme of the sermon to follow. Frequently, the preacher's theme as it is actually developed strays far afield from the announced text, but the tradition of reading a biblical verse is strong, so strong that some illiterate slave preachers of the antebellum South had their texts read for them or, lacking a Bible, pretended to read scriptural words from their hand or from a handkerchief; others claimed that, since they could not read, verses from the Bible were written by God on their hearts. The Bible is more than a source of texts; it is the single most important source of language, imagery, and story for the sermon. Through the sermon, as well as spirituals and gospel songs, the Jewish and Christian Scriptures entered and shaped the imaginative world of African-Americans. Black preachers fashioned out of the biblical characters, events, and symbols a religious ethos that fit the peculiar experience of black people in America.

After reading his text, the preacher elaborates its context. Drawing upon his knowledge of the Bible, he may range widely over both Testaments; explaining the meaning of this specific text by reference to other passages. Having set the context, the preacher ideally devotes the rest of his sermon to applying the lessons of the text to the day-to-day concerns of his congregation. Text-context-application is the conventional pattern for the development of the logic of the sermon. There is, however, another pattern as important as the structure of logical meaning, that of performance style, which gives rise to the sermon's emotive meaning.

The stylistic structure of the chanted sermon may be divided into three movements. The preacher begins calmly, speaking in conversational, if oratorical and occasionally grandiloquent, prose; he then gradually begins to speak more rapidly, excitedly, and to chant his words in time to a regular beat; finally, he reaches an emotional peak in which his chanted speech becomes tonal and merges with the singing, clapping, and shouting of the congregation. Frequently, the preacher ends the sermon by returning briefly to conversational prose.

The chanting preacher composes his sermon extemporaneously. This does not mean that he does not prepare. He may have thought about his sermon all week; he may have used a book of sermon outlines to get ideas; he may even carry notes into the pulpit. But at some point, he must breath spontaneous life into the outline, whether written or memorized, by composing on the spot a sermon delivered in rhythmic metrical speech. The meter is not based on accent but on time, the length of time between regular beats. As the preacher moves into the chanted section of his sermon, he fits his speech to a beat. When necessary, he lengthens vowels or rushes together words in order to make a line match the meter. The regularity of the beat is accentuated by the preacher's gasp for air at the end of each line. Sometimes he actually raps out the rhythm on the pulpit. The congregational responses— "Preach it, preach it," "Amen, brother," "Yes, yes, glory!"—reinforce the beat and simultaneously fill in the space left by the preacher's pause for breath. When properly "working," the rhythm of the sermon becomes "as inexorable as a drumbeat."[4]

At a certain stage, the preacher's chanting takes on a musical tone, which indicates a concomitant rise in emotional pitch. The preacher's voice changes: the timbre becomes harsh, almost hoarse. His vocal cords are constricted; his breathing is labored. All the while he moves, gestures, dances, speaking with body as well as voice.

The difficulty of delivering an extemporaneously composed metrical sermon can only be fully appreciated by one who has attempted it. The fullest description of how chanting preachers compose their sermons has been presented by Bruce Rosenberg, a medievalist interested in the composition of oral epics. Extending the theories of Parry and Lord concerning oral composition to the "art of the American folk preacher," he argues that this style of preaching is heavily formulaic. The "basic unit of composition" is, according to Rosenberg, the formula, by which he means "the metrically governed sentence" that the preacher generates in oral performance. The preacher clusters "these formulas together" into larger segments, called "themes," which become, through repetition, part of his repertoire. Since the preacher is familiar with these clusters of verses or themes, he may "fall back" upon them when his rhythm falters. Stock phrases or "stall formulas," such as C. L. Franklins's "I don't believe you hear me tonight," allow the preacher time to pause until the next verse comes to him, at the same time that they invite the congregation to respond. Because of the metrical constraints, the preacher makes frequent and effective use of repetition and tends to develop the narrative of his sermon along associational rather than logical lines.[5]

Congregational response is crucial to the delivery of the sermon. If response is weak or irregular, it will keep the preacher off stride. Conversely, if the preacher's sense of timing is poor, he will fail to rouse the congregation, and the sermon will fail. There is, then, a reciprocal relation between preacher and congregation in the composition of the sermon. Ideally, the preacher's delivery will ignite the congregation's vocal response, which will, in turn, support and push him further.

The expert preacher composes impromptu a sermon typically twenty to forty minutes in length. It is obvious that he has learned to do so only after long hours of observation and practice. However, if asked, he disavows the importance of his own skill or training in preaching and credits the sermon to the inspiration of the Holy Spirit. For this reason, chanting preachers refer to themselves as "spiritual" preachers as distinct from "manuscript" preachers, that is, those who read their sermons from prepared texts. In this view, the preacher's words are placed in his mind and on his lips by the Holy Spirit. The preacher is literally the instrument of God's breath, "God's trombone," in James Weldon Johnson's apt metaphor. When the preacher states that he is "filled with" or "set on fire by the Spirit," he is not only claiming that he is a channel of God's grace or that God is telling him what to say; he is also describing his own ecstatic experience of preaching. As he preaches, he feels that a force or power other than his ordinary self takes over.

This power he identifies as the Spirit of God. Hence the conventional antipathy of the "old-time preacher" to formal seminary training—"I haven't rubbed my head on seminary walls"—was only partially due to the suspicion that education would alienate him from his uneducated flock. The insistence that the sermon was God's work, not man's, tended to undermine the importance of education for preaching. Two other conventions stem from the same rationale: the preacher's contention that he resisted God's call to preach until it proved irresistible and his frequent complaint as he steps to the pulpit: "I feel poorly this morning." In both cases, the weakness of the minister and the strength of God are acclaimed.

Similarly, the members of the congregation explain that the emotional experience that moves them to sing, shout, and dance is the effect of God's Spirit. The experiential claims of the preacher and his congregation should not be dismissed as conventional piety. Rather, they should be taken seriously by those who want to understand the sermon, precisely because these claims of inspiration define and determine the expectations and so the performances of both preacher and congregation. The experiential dimension is crucial because for Evangelical Christians one only becomes Christian through an *experience*, the experience of conversion. And even after conversion, religion has to be vital, "heartfelt," and not just intellectually convincing. When religious fervor grows cold, it is time for revival.

Early descriptions of Methodist and Baptist preaching, black and white, suggest three characteristics: it was plain or simple in language, dramatic in delivery, and—at least for the Baptists—musical, if we can believe the pejorative description applied by their critics: "Baptist whine." Today's chanted sermon still evidences these traits. The preacher's eloquence is measured not by his book learning but by his mother-wit. Down-home familiarity, wordplay, humor, well-turned phrases put a congregation at ease and encourage them to identify with the preacher. Formal, academic, scholarly language is inappropriate. It is viewed as "lecturing" not preaching and leaves the congregation cold. Dramatic ability, as much as sense of timing, is a necessity for the successful preacher, who may play several parts at once in the pulpit as he retells one of the familiar Bible stories. The relation of music and preaching has been symbiotic. There is a vocal continuum between speech and song in the sermon, as speech becomes rhythmic chant, and chant in turn becomes tonal and shades into song. The sermon may be introduced and closed by a hymn. Preachers make extensive use of verses from spiritual and hymns within their sermons. Conversely, gospel quartets and rhythm-and-blues singers imitate the style of the chanting preacher.

The date of the first chanted sermon cannot be given, because there was, of course, no such moment. Many sermons and many influences contributed to the development of this sermonic style: the emphasis placed upon biblical preaching by Evangelical Protestantism, the emotional and dramatic delivery legitimated by the Great Awakening of the mid eighteenth century, the ecstatic behavior encouraged by the revivals, the musical "tuned" voice of early Baptist preachers, the antiphonal pattern familiarized by the custom of lining-out hymns, and the renewed stress upon Christian experience fostered by American revivalism. By the early decades of the nineteeth century, the chanted sermon had probably emerged as a recognizable style of preaching. At midcentury Frederick Olmsted observed and described a chanted sermon delivered in a black church in New Orleans:

> As soon as I had taken my seat, my attention was attracted by an old negro near me, whom I supposed for some time to be suffering under some nervous complaint; he trembled, his teeth chattered, and his face, at intervals, was convulsed. He soon began to respond aloud to the sentiments of the preacher, in such words as these: "Oh, yes,!" and similar expressions could be heard from all parts of the house whenever the speaker's voice was unusually solemn, or his language and manner eloquent or excited.
>
> Sometimes the outcries and responses were not confined to ejaculations of this kind, but shouts, and groans, terrific shrieks, and indescribable expressions of ecstasy—of pleasure or agony—and even stamping, jumping, and clapping of hands were added.... I was once surprised to find my own muscles all stretched, as if ready for a struggle—my face glowing, and my feet stamping—having been infected unconsciously.... I could not, when my mind reverted to itself, find any connection or meaning in the phrases of the speaker that remained in my memory; and I have no doubt it was his "action" rather than his sentiments, that had given rise to the excitement of the congregation.[6]

Olmsted's description focuses on the power of the sermon to excite ecstatic response, even in a cultured white northerner like Olmsted himself.

Mary Boykin Chesnut, a southern white woman, found herself excited by the chanted style with which a slave driver on her plantation delivered a prayer:

> He became wildly excited, on his knees, facing us with his eyes shut. He clapped his hands at the end of every sentence, and his voice rose to the pitch of a shrill shriek, yet was strangely clear and musical, occasionally in a plaintive minor key that went to your heart. Sometimes it rang out like a trumpet. I wept bitterly.... The Negroes sobbed and shouted and swayed backward and forward,

some with aprons to their eyes, most of them clapping their hands
and responding in shrill tones: "Yes, God!" "Jesus?" "Savior?"
"Bless de Lord, amen," etc. It was a little too exciting for me. I
would very much have liked to shout, too.... When he rose from
his knees [he] trembled and shook as one in a palsy, and from his
eyes you could see the ecstasy had not left him yet.[7]

In both instances, the observers distinguish the style of delivery
from the meaning of the sermon or, in Chesnut's case, prayer. Both
find themselves moved, but neither considers the possibility that
the ecstasy they resist is itself the meaning of the events they witness. By dismissing the "sense" of the emotional behavior aroused
by the style of the sermon or prayer, Olmsted and Chesnut are
missing the message. The same mistake is made by the modern
observer who separates form from content, style from meaning in
describing the chanted sermon. To identify ecstatic behavior with
the style of the preacher, and instruction or edification with the
intelligible content of his words, is to misunderstand the com-
plexity of the sermon and the religious ethos from which it
springs.

Ecstatic religious behavior is central to the religious tradition
in which the chanting preacher stands. As we have seen, the
origins of this tradition can be found in the Evangelical revivals of
the eighteenth and nineteenth centuries. But there is another
source not yet mentioned: the African religious culture of the
slaves. A look at this distant heritage and its interaction with Protestant revivalism may help to explain how style and meaning are
one in the sermon and why it is that the chanted delivery has ex-
erted such a long and deep appeal. In the revivals, African-
Americans found a context in which the bodily expression of religious emotion was not only permitted but encouraged—hark-
ing back to the danced religions of their African forebears. Black
American Christians were filled with the Spirit of the Christian
God, but they responded in ways markedly similar to the ways

in which their ancestors had responded to possession by the gods of Africa. Possessed by the Holy Spirit, slaves and freedmen danced, sang, and shouted in styles that were African. More important, ecstatic trance was at the center of their worship as it had been in Africa. In the revivals, African and Christian traditions met on common ground, ecstatic response to divine possession. The African tradition of religious dance was Christianized and the Evangelical Protestant tradition of experiential religion was Africanized.[8]

The influence of African traditions upon the religious dancing and singing of slaves and their descendants may be granted, but what about preaching? Where does the African influence lie? Anthropologist Morton Marks has suggested an answer. According to Marks, there is a ritual structure underlying several kinds of speech events within African-American cultures in the New World. The structure consists of an alternation from European styles of performance to African ones. When the style switch occurs, it acts as a code signaling that ritual possession by the Spirit is about to occur. To the observer unfamiliar with the performance clues, the stylistic switch is commonly perceived as a change from order to chaos, from music to noise, or from speech to gibberish. What in fact is really happening is a shift from one type of order to another: from a nonrhythmic to a rhythmic, or rather, increasingly rhythmic, performance style. The importance of rhythmic drumming and singing for the onset of divine possession in African and African-American religions has been widely observed. Applied to the chanted sermon, Marks's theory implies that the preacher's switch from conversational prose to the metrical and tonal chant, the rhythm holding steady as a drumbeat, sets the stage for the divine possession that everyone expects. Moreover there are recognizable cues that announce the Spirit's arrival. The preacher's harsh vocal sound, the constriction of voice, the audible gasp at the end of each line, the tonal quality, the participatory claps, shouts and noise of the congregation all announce the onset of possession and instigate it in others. In this sense, the preacher's style itself speaks, at least to those who understand the language of his sermonic tradition.[9]

Admittedly, Marks's theory is an interpretation; it has not been proved. Still the notion that African-influenced performance styles have been transmitted to American blacks and that they are shared across different African-American cultures in the New World has been convincingly demonstrated for dance, song, and music. It may very well be true of the chanted sermon and other forms of oral performance as well.

The chanted sermon is the product of a religious imagination in which experience is primary and is so because it validates religious truth. Without experience, how can one know that one's religious life is real? In the words of one former slave: "Nobody can talk about the religion of God unless they've had a religious experience in it."[10] In the chanted sermon, African-American Christians did not merely talk about God, they experienced his power, and found that in the experience their own spirits were renewed.

Chapter Eight

The Conversion Experience

IN HIS CLASSIC ESSAY "The Faith of the Fathers," published in *Souls of Black Folk* (1903), W. E. B. Du Bois distinguished three characteristics of black religion: the preacher, the sorrow songs, and the "frenzy" or ecstasy. He might well have added a fourth, the experience of conversion, an experience central to Evangelical Protestantism, the predominant tradition of African-American Christians, whether Baptist, Methodist, or Holiness-Pentecostal. Events of great psychological, social, and cultural power, conversion experiences have transformed the lives of generations of black Americans since the days of slavery.

Conversion, literally a "turning," is an ancient and perennial concept in Christian piety that ultimately derives from Christianity's origins in Judaism. The biblical Prophets' calls to Israel to turn from sin to God, as well as the rhetorical power of their exhortations, served as models for Christian preachers and congregations for centuries, inspiring the long-lived sermonic tradition of the jeremiad as well as supplying countless texts, images, and exempla for the unceasing effort of the Church to change people's attitudes and values. Conversion represented not just a change in behavior but *metanoia*, a change of heart, a transformation in consciousness—a radical reorientation of personality, exemplified in the stories of St. Paul the Apostle and St. Augustine of Hippo as a life-changing event brought about by the direct intervention of

God. The development of Christian monasticism in the deserts of late antique Egypt and Syria and its spread to the West introduced the life of asceticism and contemplation as the standard of conversion par excellence.

The medieval church tended to identify the divine call to change one's life with the act of entering a monastic or mendicant religious order. This apparent restriction of the conversion to a "professional" class of religious prompted late medieval church reformers to reaffirm conversion as the vocation of all Christians, no matter their station in life. Martin Luther's tower experience of conversion and his theological elaboration of it as "justification by faith alone" became the cornerstone for the sixteenth-century Reformation's recovery of the experience of conversion as a normative stage in the life of each Christian. Promulgated in the English Reformation, particularly by the Puritans, this experiential emphasis led to an inward-looking piety that rejected wholesale the external ritualism of the unreformed church in favor of attending closely to the inner workings of God's spirit upon the Christian heart. So seriously did Puritans take the matter, that in New England, free to establish their own church order, they required individuals to render an account of their conversion experiences as a qualification for full membership in the church. As we've seen, the spread of the Baptists and the Methodists during the late eighteenth and early nineteenth centuries institutionalized a conversion-oriented, revival-based piety in the South and shaped the form of Christianity that the slaves increasingly made their own. By the 1770s slave converts were exercising their own gifts, and sometimes whites as well as blacks experienced conversion under their preaching.

The predominant themes of the Evangelical tradition concerning conversion were echoed in African-American conversion narratives: the expectation of a conversion experience as a necessary step to becoming a church member, the incapacity of the soul before the power of sin, the sovereignty of God as demonstrated by the irresistable power of divine grace to work a transformation in the sinner's life. And yet these accounts echo other traditions as well. Africans and their descendants in Protestant America discovered analogues in revivalistic Evangelicalism to the religious beliefs and rituals of Africa, which turned out to be crucial for the process of reinterpretation that made Christianity intelligible and adaptable for large numbers of African-Americans. Rituals of initiation in many African societies, including induction into adulthood, into secret societies, and into service of the spirits, regularly incorporated death and rebirth symbols that were entirely consonant with the central symbolism of Christian conversion as regeneration. Moreover, as we have seen, the ecstatic behavior widely associated with revivals—such outward expression of the Spirit's inner promptings as shouting, clapping, and dancing—mirrored the singing, dancing, and drumming in ceremonies of possession trance that regularly manifested the presence of the divine in many African religions. Similarly, growing ill, loss of appetite, debility of any sort, clear indications of sin-sickness for an Evangelical Protestant, were commonly interpreted by Africans as warnings from the spirits for one to mend his or her ways or as a call from a god to undergo initiation into divine service. A tantalizing hint of the translations slaves made between African and Christian concepts of religious initiation was left by Henry Brown, a slave in Virginia, who observed that it was the custom of slaves on his plantation to shave their heads when they became anxious about the state of their souls.[1] Shaving the head is a common custom in Yoruba- and Dahomean-derived religions to prepare the initiate for reception of a divine spirit.

Many African-American conversion accounts mention a private praying ground, located in thickets, woods, bushes, or at a particular tree, to which the anxious sinner retreats to beg mercy, often at night. In many African societies, the bush is widely believed to be the place for initiation because it is the place where spirits dwell and night is the time to meet them. The identity of the mysterious "little man" who occurs in so many of the conversion visions has prompted a great deal of speculation, including the suggestion that he is related to the trickster figure, variously identified in West Africa, who not only puts people to the test, but also "opens the way" as messenger between the gods and human beings. Could this little man, who appears at moments of trial and danger to guide the sinner to the path of salvation, represent the transposition of an African god with a similar function into a very similar role within a Christian conversion experience? Whatever the answer to this question, it is clear that the slaves fashioned out of several religious traditions, African derived as well as Evangelical Christian, a coherent vision of religious initiation that became normative for the vast majority of black Christians.

Reading the conversion narratives of African-Americans, one is immediately struck by the vividness of the imagery and its similarity from one account to the next. A common store of biblical sources, especially the Book of Revelation, helps to explain the frequency with which the same images appear. These were common cultural images, heard over and over again in hymns and prayers and expounded upon in sermon after sermon. The accounts also betray a common narrative pattern as a result of the regular recitation of conversion experiences at revivals and "experience meetings" by the converted, who were expected to talk about the working of the Spirit upon their hearts. Individual and unique as these conversion experiences were, they shared the common narrative construction and group norms associated with the tradition. Thus conversion was both a profoundly personal experience and an experience defined and validated within a community of church folk.

The communal and liturgical contexts of conversion are crucial elements of the experience itself. And the influence of preachers, church elders, and parents upon the narrator's conversion constitutes an indispensable interpersonal dimension. Indeed, communal guidance and validation were built into the process of conversion called "seeking" by the elderly black church folk of low-country South Carolina and Georgia. Seeking typically began in adolescence with a spiritual experience that drove a young person to become serious about salvation. Young women would then be directed by the Holy Spirit to a "spiritual mother," young men to a "spiritual father." The spiritual mother or father, who typically had already been informed by the Spirit to expect a seeker, agreed to act as a guide over the weeks or even months that the process might last. These elders, experienced in the ways of the Lord, interpreted the dreams and visions of seekers, offered instruction and support, and finally informed them when they were ready to go before the church to render an account of God's action and their response. The inner experience of the seeker typically involved visions and dream travel. Required to pray at dawn, noon, sunset, and midnight, often in the midst of a wood or thicket, seekers were supposed to follow wherever the Spirit led and to report all dreams and visions to their guides. When the spiritual mother or father deemed the time was right, the seeker appeared before the elders of the congregation, and if the testimony was accepted, the young person was given the right hand of fellowship as a sign of welcome to membership in the church. If the testimony was rejected, the seeker was sent back to seek some more.[2] It may be that this elaborate and traditional initiation process was geographically restricted to the low country, but I suspect that some form of seeking was a familiar process across many African-American communities. At any rate, conversion was a major social method for initiating adolescents into the community for generations of African-Americans. In the process, black children endured the pressure of adult expectation, but they also enjoyed the encouragement, guidance, and affirmation of their elders.

At base, conversion involved a deeply personal experience of direction, orientation, and validation. The vividness of the imagery of their accounts attests to the profound appropriation of the biblical symbols by the narrators. In effect, their individual biographies became sacralized by casting them against the backdrop of the age-old cosmic struggle between the benevolence of God and the malevolence of evil. The resonances of this sacred drama upon the daily conditions of the rest of their lives should not be underestimated. When the narrators spoke of their conversion as a rebirth, of being made entirely new, of being filled with love for everything and everybody, they revealed the depth of internal transformation that defined their identity and self-worth. For those facing the dehumanizing conditions of enslavement—the daily physical, psychological, and emotional attacks against one's dignity as a person—to experience the total acceptance and affirmation of self by God challenged the mentality of slavery at a fundamental level. In the conversion experience slaves realized—and realized it in the heart not just the head—that they were of infinite value as children of God, chosen from all eternity to be saved. Within a system bent on reducing them to a status of utter inferiority, the experience of conversion rooted deep within the slave converts' psyche a sense of personal value and individual importance that helped to ground their identity in the unimpeachable authority of almighty God. Returning to this experience, as they did regularly in prayer meetings and worship services, former slaves and their descendants fashioned a powerful defense of their humanity. They knew that they constituted, in James Baldwin's fine phrase, a "spiritual aristocracy" who did not simply talk about God's Word, but experienced its power on the altars of their hearts. Despite their oppression, they adapted from the religious resources available to them a ritual of *metonoia* that made it possible for them not only to deny the brutal limits of slavery, but to transcend them.

James Baldwin's *Go Tell It on the Mountain* offers one of the most profound depictions of the conversion experience as progression from suffering to transcendence. With great moral sensitivity, psychological verisimilitude, and emotional power, Baldwin develops the story of the conversion of John Grimes into a proclamation about the meaning of black history and the mystery of human suffering.

In the first chapter of the novel, something happens that will serve as an emblem for the meaning of the entire narrative to follow. As John Grimes grudgingly obeys his mother's request to clean the livingroom on his fourteenth birthday, his eyes fall upon a group of objects randomly arranged on the mantelpiece:

> The mantelpiece held, in brave confusion, photographs, greeting cards, flowered mottoes, two silver candlesticks that held no candles, and a green metal serpent, poised to strike.... One of the mottoes was pink and blue, and proclaimed in raised letters, which made the work of dusting harder:
>
> *Come in the evening, or come in the morning,*
> *Come when you're looked for, or come without warning,*
> *A thousand welcomes you'll find here before you,*
> *And the oftener you come here, the more we'll adore you.*
>
> And the other, in letters of fire against a background of gold, stated:
>
> *For God so loved the world, that He gave His only begotten Son,*
> *that whosoever should believe in Him should not perish, but*
> *have everlasting life.*
>
> John 3:16

These somewhat unrelated sentiments decorated either side of the mantelpiece, obscured a little by the silver candlesticks. Between these two extremes, the greeting cards, received year after year, on Christmas, or Easter, or birthdays, trumpeted their glad tidings; while the green metal serpent, perpetually malevolent, raised its head proudly in the midst of these trophies, biding the time to strike. Against the mirror, like a procession, the photographs were arranged.[3]

The distance between the two "somewhat unrelated sentiments" represents the spiritual, psychological, and emotional distance that John Grimes will travel on this day of his birth and rebirth. On the one hand, the sentimental attitude of childhood faith
sigfnified by the pink and blue motto, on the other, the core message of the Christian gospel, etched in "letters of fire against a
background of gold," the colors of the fire-baptism that will seal
John's transformation to adult faith in the climactic closing section
of the novel, "the threshing floor." A journey from innocence to
experience for reader as well as John Grimes, a journey achieved
only through suffering.

Between these emblematic mottoes stand the greeting cards
representing the seasons, the passage of years, and the photographs, the history of John Grimes's people, whose stories we will
learn in the middle section of the book "the prayer of the saints."
And, significantly, in the midst of this history stands the ever-
malevolent serpent poised to strike.

At one level, *Go Tell It on the Mountain* is the story of John
Grimes's conversion, his coming to accept the faith of his Pentecostal family and community; at another level, it is the story of his
acceptance of the history of his people and his incorporation into
the experience of black Americans. At the beginning he seeks to
escape both, seeing the misery, the poverty, and the blighted lives
that racism and segregation have created, especially the bitterness
that has corroded his stepfather, Gabriel. John, a bright student
whose ability is appreciated by his teachers, sees an opportunity
to break out of the straitjacket of his stepfather's hatred of whites.
He dreams of success in the great "broadway" of the white world.

Standing on a favorite hill in Central Park, John is taken with
the allure of ambition, the dream of success and the wealth in the
city.[4] Baldwin uses the scene to allude to the temptation of Christ
by Satan, who takes him to the top of a tall mountain and shows
him all the kingdoms of the world, promising him dominion over

all if he will simply bow down and adore him. The scene also alludes to the triumphal entrance of Jesus into Jerusalem riding upon the foal of a donkey—an entrance not of a conquering victor but of a meek and humble "king," whose victory will be achieved through his own defeat and death. In each case, power as the world defines it is rejected for a radically different kind of power, a power of spirit and of truth. Contasting the proud towers of Manhattan with the squat tenements of Harlem, John longs to escape but is brought up short by the biblical injunction: broad is the way to perdition, narrow the path to salvation. He yearns to escape the constriction and squalor of his peoples' lives, the burden of their history, and yet he intuits that it is not salvation, but damnation that lies in that direction. At this stage of the novel and of John's own consciousness, the condemnation of the broad way seems to stem from the asceticism of John's religious upbringing in a Pentecostal church. But Baldwin is implying in this passage a broader assertion about the meaning of power, wealth, poverty, and suffering, which will become explicit for John and for us as the book draws to an end.

In addition to religious and racial questions, John Grimes is struggling with a set of conflicts that include the antagonism between himself and his stepfather, his sexual attraction to his friend Elisha, and his internalized image of himself as ugly. All of these problems of identity will be "winnowed" in his conversion experience on the threshing floor. John's identity, however, is not merely personal; it is transpersonal insofar as it rests in an interlocking web of relationships with those relatives whose lives have gone into making John and his circumstances. Though he does not realize it, the stories of Gabriel, Elizabeth, and Florence—each of them tragic—form the background to his struggle and each in its own way culminates in his attempt to "come through," just as the "prayers of the saints" converge around the mourner, assisting him to pass through the pangs of rebirth.

In the stories of Gabriel, Elizabeth, and Florence, moreover, Baldwin encapsulates the history of black Americans, from the post-Emancipation rural South to the urban ghetto of the twentieth-century great migration. And he does so in language that masterfully echoes the images and cadences of the preaching, praying, and singing of black religion, effectively casting his narrative in the religious idiom that African-Americans have predominantly used to define their history. Shadowed by racial oppression and violence from without, the lives of John's family are riven from within by jealousy, pride, misunderstanding, and the failure to love. Their stories come to a focus upon him as he is struck down by the Spirit, struggling on the dusty floor of a storefront church in Harlem. He falls not only under the weight of sin, but under the burden of the accumulated history of suffering inflicted upon his people.

It is precisely this suffering that John seeks to escape. He desperately wants to flee the misery and poverty and oppression of this company of "niggers." And so the reasonable voice urging him to get up off the floor, to reject this experience, seems to remind him of his exceptional promise and ambition for achievement. But the more he struggles, the deeper he falls; there is no escape, except to go through. John is being claimed by a spiritual force larger than his own ego, a force that pushes him onto an archetypal journey across an ancient landscape, populated by prophets, apostles, and martyrs.

In his trance he confronts an army of people. Puzzled at first, he comes to understand whose company it is that he seeks so desperately to flee. They are the wretched of the earth, the poor, the oppressed, those who suffer. And he is in their company; there will be no escape. Their sufferings will be his. Suddenly suffering becomes a sound—a sound "he had heard all his life, but it was only now that his ears were open to this sound that came from darkness, that could only come from darkness, that yet bore such sure witness to the glory of the light."⁵ This sound was identical to the sound of Mother McCanless's tambourine, the sound that filled her testimony with such unimpeachable authority. This sound John not only recognizes but now internalizes:

And now in his moaning, and so far from any help, he heard it in himself—it rose from his bleeding, his cracked-open heart. It was a sound of rage and weeping which filled the grave, rage and weeping from time set free, but bound now in eternity; rage that had no language, weeping with no voice—which yet spoke now, to John's startled soul, of boundless melancholy, of the bitterest patience, and the longest night; of the deepest water, the strongest chains, the most cruel lash; of humility most wretched, the dungeon most absolute, of love's bed defiled, and birth dishonored, and most bloody, unspeakable, sudden death. Yes, the darkness hummed with murder: the body in the water, the body in the fire, the body on the tree. John looked down the line of these armies of darkness, army upon army, and his soul whispered: *Who are these? Who are they?* And wondered: *Where shall I go?*⁶

John struggles to escape "out of this darkness, out of this company—into the land of the living, so high, so far away." But he finds no escape And in his desperate fear calls out to the Lord for mercy. He hears for the first time in his struggle a voice that whispers to him "Go Through," "Ask Him to take you through." "And he saw before him the fire, red and gold, and burning in a night eternal, and waiting for him. He must go through this fire, and into this night." Then John glimpses, "for a moment only," the Lord; "and the darkness, for a moment only, was filled with a light he could not bear." And in that moment he was set free. "The light and the darkness had kissed each other, and were married now, forever, in the life and the vision of John's soul."⁷

John has been transformed. He has been transformed not by fleeing his peoples' history but by identifying with that history, by permitting himself to be grasped by it. And in being grasped, engulfed by that company of suffering, he comes to comprehend the paradox that it is precisely these wretched of the earth who are the chosen ones of God. He finds himself, in their company, joining the long line of prophets, apostles, and martyrs of biblical tradition, in the company of those who constitute a "spiritual aristocracy." Complementing the earlier vision of the suffering, violent, and bloody history of black Americans, now comes another vision. In a passage redolent of Scripture, spirituals, gospel song, and sermons, Baldwin reads in John Grimes's experience the paradoxical history of suffering and triumph of those who have gone before.

No power could hold this army back, no water disperse them, no fire consume them. One day they would compel the earth to heave upward, and surrender the waiting dead. They sang, where the darkness gathered, where the lion waited, where the fire cried, and where the blood ran down:

My soul, don't you be uneasy!

They wandered in the valley forever; and they smote the rock, forever; and the waters sprang, perpetually, in the perpetual desert. They cried unto the Lord forever, and lifted up their eyes forever, they were cast down forever, and He lifted them up forever. No, the fire could not hurt them, and yes, the lion's jaws were stopped; the serpent was not their master, the grave was not their resting-place, the earth was not their home. Job bore them witness, and Abraham was their father. Moses had elected to suffer with them rather than glory in sin for a season. Shadrach, Meshach, and Abednego had gone before them into the fire, their grief had been sung by David, and Jeremiah had wept for them. Ezekiel had prophesied upon them, these scattered bones, these slain, and, in the fulness of time, the prophet, John, had come out of the wilderness, crying that the promise was for them. They were encompassed with a very cloud of witnesses: Judas, who had betrayed the Lord; Thomas, who had doubted Him; Peter, who had trembled at the crowing of a cock; Stephen, who had been stoned; Paul, who had been bound; the blind man crying in the dusty road, the dead man rising from the grave. And they looked unto Jesus, the author and the finisher of their faith, running with patience the race He had set before them; they endured the cross, and they despised the shame, and waited to join Him, one day, in glory, at the right hand of the Father.[8]

In this striking passage Baldwin conflates African-American history with biblical salvation-history just as black Americans have done since at least the early nineteenth century in language that echoes the idiom of their religious culture.

The gospel to be "told on the mountain," then, is the lesson of black history itself, that salvation lies not in the high road of the proud and the mighty but with the poor, the suffering, the wretched of the earth. It is these rejected ones who are the chosen people of God, the New Israel, the Redeemer Nation, not merely because they suffer—that would be masochism on a grand scale—but because they achieve the moral and emotional strength to draw out of their pain profound lessons about human life, truths that can only be learned through suffering. Suffering, Baldwin says, can be transformed into a source of wisdom and strength; it can reveal the inner resources of the person; or as Martin Luther King would put it, "suffering can be redemptive."

In a secular rather than sacred idiom, Baldwin rephrases this motif in the autobiographical essay "Down at the Cross: Letter from a Region in My Mind," published in *The Fire Next Time.* Here he argues that America has much to learn from the experience of her black citizens, especially that to place one's trust in might and wealth and power is to fall within the grip of a dangerous illusion. Fragility, suffering, and death are the human condition and must be accepted if people are to achieve maturity and authenticity. In language strikingly similar to the passage quoted above from *Go Tell It on the Mountain,* Baldwin reflects on the meaning of the black past:

This past, the Negro's past, of rope, fire, torture, castration, infanticide, rape; death and humiliation; fear by day and night, fear as deep as the marrow of the bone; doubt that he was worthy of life, since everyone around him denied it; sorrow for his women, for his kinfolk, for his children, who needed his protection, and whom he could not protect; rage, hatred, and murder, hatred for white men so deep that it often turned against him and his own, and made all love, all trust, all joy impossible—this past, this endless struggle to achieve and reveal and confirm a human identity, human authority, yet contains, for all its horror, something very beautiful. I do not mean to be sentimental about suffering—enough is certainly as good as a feast—but people who cannot suffer can never grow up, can never discover who they are. That man who is forced each day to snatch his manhood, his identity, out of the fire of human cruelty that rages to destroy it knows, if he survives his effort, and even if he does not survive it, something about himself and human life that no school on earth—and, indeed, no church—can teach. He achieves his own authority, and that is unshakable.[9]

Certain experiences in life cannot be circumvented, but must be "gone through," if one is to learn who one is. And yet massive denial of who we are surrounds us at every turn. This denial *is* the serpent, the original tempter, the "father of lies," who leads people to reject their identity, to demean their value, to internalize racism, to yield to forces bent on reducing them to less than their full worth as persons. The serpent is bent on "striking down" our souls. The serpent is the impulse that takes John to the mountaintop in Central Park and promises him all the kingdoms of the world if he will only reject his past, his people, and so his identity. It is the serpent's ironic voice that tells him to get up off the threshing floor because he doesn't belong with these niggers. It is the serpent who would tempt us all to choose the unreality of power and the illusion of wealth over truth, responsibility, and compassion. He waits in the midst of all our lives, perpetually malevolent, ready to strike.

Chapter Nine

A Hidden Wholeness: Thomas Merton
and Martin Luther King, Jr.

AT THE TIME OF HIS ASSASSINATION, plans were underway for
Martin Luther King, Jr., to make a retreat with Thomas Merton
at Our Lady of Gethsemani Abbey. We shall never know what
might have resulted from a dialogue between this Roman Catholic
monk and this black Baptist preacher whose lives still fascinate
and inspire us twenty-five years after their deaths. But the act
of recalling their common struggle against the evils of racism,
materialism, and militarism may enable us to recover what they
would have brought to such an encounter and to imagine the joint
"word" they might have left those who strive to live out their
legacy.[1]

They came, of course, from two very different backgrounds. A
quick comparison of their biographies would seem to demonstrate
that the only thing that Father Louis Merton, O.C.S.O., and the
Reverend Dr. Martin Luther King, Jr., held in common was the
year of their deaths— 1968. Merton was born in Prades, France,
in 1915, the son of Owen Merton, an artist from New Zealand,
and Ruth Jenkins Merton, an artist from the United States. His
mother died when Merton was only six, and his father when he
was fifteen. His childhood and adolescence were unsettled. Shut-
tling between France, England, Bermuda, and Long Island, New
York, Merton experienced the homelessness of the expatriate, the

rootlessness of the transient adrift in an uncaring world, and the longing of the orphan for family stability. Educated at European boarding schools, at Cambridge, and at Columbia between the two world wars, Merton experienced the disillusionment with the modern world that many of the intellectuals of his generation felt. His conversion to Roman Catholicism incorporated him into a firmly established system of values and doctrines that countered the anomie and hedonism he deplored in modern society. "Leaving the world," he would find both a home and a family in the community life of a Cistercian monastery in Kentucky.[2]

From his parents Merton absorbed the temperament of the artist, though his talent expressed itself in writing, not painting. This artistic perspective tended to nurture in him a critical distance from the world. Fortunately, Merton's superiors recognized and encouraged his vocation as a writer, and throughout his years in the monastery he remained an amazingly prolific author, publishing more than forty-eight books of poetry, essays, biography, autobiography, journals, meditations, and social criticism. Writing requires discipline and solitude. The strictly regulated life of a contemplative monk offered the disciplined structure Merton needed, and he himself helped persuade his order to recover the value of solitude in its own tradition by reinstituting the practice of allowing some monks to become hermits. He lived the last years of his life in a hermitage. Illustrating the theological adage "Grace builds on nature," Merton's distanced perspective upon the world and his need for disciplined solitude, derived from his "expatriate" past and from his sensibilities as a literary artist, were deepened, fulfilled, and—as we shall see—transformed by the contemplative tradition in which he immersed himself.

Martin Luther King, Jr., was born in Atlanta in 1929, the son of Alberta Williams King and Martin Luther King, Sr., pastor of Ebenezer Baptist Church. Compared to Merton's, King's childhood was a happy and secure one, though all too early he was made aware of the hurts inflicted by racism.³ Like his father, grandfather, and great-grandfather, King entered the ministry, and throughout the years of his leadership in the civil rights movement, he would remain a preacher, drawing upon the black church tradition in which he was formed for both the style and content of his message. Courses in philosophy, ethics, and theology at Morehouse College, Crozier Seminary, and Boston University provided King with the opportunity to develop an intellectual framework for systematic analysis of the relationship between Christianity and society, but the existential base for King's commitment to social action was already established in the tradition of black religious protest. Certainly the intellectual sources commonly credited with influencing King's development—Thoreau's doctrine of noncooperation with evil, Rauschenbusch's social gospel, Gandhi's nonviolence, and the philosophical school of personalism at Boston University—were important, but so was the example of his father, who in 1935 had led several thousand black demonstrators in support of voting rights for black citizens, and his maternal grandfather, the Reverend Adam Daniel Williams, who ten years earlier had organized demonstrations to protest a municipal bond issue that made no provisions for high-school education for black students.⁴

Strongly attracted to the intellectual life, King might very well have followed the example of Benjamin Mays or Howard Thurman by combining ministerial and academic careers. He could have taught in a seminary in the North and we might today be reading his texts in social ethics, but he decided instead that the place for him was a pastorate in the South. And so he accepted that fateful call to pastor the Dexter Avenue Baptist Church.

Our Lady of Gethsemani Abbey and Dexter Avenue Baptist Church, Catholic monasticism and black Protestantism—two very different locations and two very different traditions that nevertheless held one significant trait in common, their marginality. Monks were marginal by profession; they had rejected the "world." Blacks were marginalized by discrimination; they were rejected by the dominant white society. Both monasticism and the black church were profoundly extraneous to the priorities and values of America in the 1950s. Marginality provided Merton and King with the critical consciousness necessary for radical dissent from the religious and political status quo. Moreover, the contemplative tradition within monasticism and the prophetic tradition within African-American religion furnished Merton, the contemplative, and King, the prophet, with the spiritual insight necessary to articulate convincing critical analyses of society and the religious experience necessary to ground their prescriptions for social change in personal authenticity.

Yet it was not the traditions per se, but what King and Merton took from them, or better, the ways in which King and Merton were transformed by them, that made all the difference. Initially, neither Merton nor King set out to "save the soul of the nation," as King's SCLC would later put it. There was in the young Merton the enthusiasm of the convert, which led him to espouse in his earlier works, like *The Seven Storey Mountain* (1948), a world-rejecting attitude that he later came to recant:

> The contemplative life is not [he wrote in 1964], and cannot be, a mere withdrawal, a pure negation, a turning of one's back on the world with its suffering, its crises, its confusions and its errors. First of all, the attempt itself would be illusory. No man can withdraw completely from the society of his fellow men; and the monastic community is deeply implicated, for better or for worse, in the economic, political, and social structures of the contemporary world.[5]

We are all, according to Merton, in the fine phrase he used to entitle one of his published journals, "guilty bystanders." The Merton who had written a series of widely read "modern spiritual classics"—*Seeds of Contemplation* (1949), *The Ascent to Truth*

(1951), *Bread in the Wilderness* (1953), *The Living Bread* (1956), *Thoughts in Solitude* (1958)—was suddenly turning out volumes of essays on civil rights, nuclear weapons, the Vietnam War, and expressing radical views on social and political issues. No doubt the change in Merton was due in part to maturity, the deromanticization of monastic life, the recovery of earlier concerns about race and peace, but it was also due to his deepening understanding of the vocation of the monk and the meaning of contemplation. The change was probably gradual, but Merton interpreted it in his journals as a revelatory experience. One of the most famous passages in Merton's writing, it is worth quoting extensively:

> In Louisville, at the corner of Fourth and Walnut, in the center of the shopping district, I was suddenly overwhelmed with the realization that I loved all these people, that they were mine and I theirs, that we could not be alien to one another even though we were total strangers. It was like waking from a dream of separateness, of spurious self-isolation in a special world, the world of renunciation and supposed holiness. The whole illusion of a separate holy existence is a dream. Not that I question the reality of my vocation, or of my monastic life: but the conception of "separation from the world" that we have in the monastery too easily presents itself as a complete illusion.... We are in the same world as everybody else, the world of the bomb, the world of race hatred, the world of technology, the world of mass media, big business, revolution, and all the rest.... This sense of liberation from an illusory difference was such a relief and such a joy to me that I almost laughed out loud. . . . To think that for sixteen or seventeen years I have been taking seriously this pure illusion that is implicit in so much of our monastic thinking. . . . I have the immense joy of being a man, a member of a race in which God Himself became incarnate. As if the sorrows and stupidities of the human condition could overwhelm me, now I realize what we all are. And if only everybody could realize this! But it cannot be explained. There is no way of telling people that they are all walking around shining like the sun.[6]

Merton went on to assert that it was the particular task of the monk to speak out of his silence and solitude with an independent voice in order to clarify for those who were "completely immersed in other cares" the true value of the human person amid the illusions with which mass society surrounds modern man at every turn. The contemplative then has a responsibility to dissent, lest by his forgetfulness, ignorance, and silence he actually complies with what he thinks he has left behind. In a profoundly paradoxical statement, Merton claims: "My solitude, however, is not my own, for I see now how much it belongs to them—and that I have a responsibility for it in their regard, not just in my own. It is because I am one with them that I owe it to them to be alone, and when I am alone they are not 'they' but my own self. There are no strangers!"[7]

King's life, like Merton's, was turned from its expected trajectory by an unexpected event. That event was the 1955 Montgomery bus boycott, which King had neither started nor suggested, but which irrevocably changed him from the successful pastor of a moderately comfortable church to the leader of a national movement for racial justice.[8] As spokesman for the boycott, King was overwhelmed with a load of backbreaking responsibilities and frightened by threats against his life and his family. Reaching the end of his endurance, King sat at his kitchen table one night over a cup of coffee, trying to figure out how to get out of the movement without appearing a coward.

And I discovered then that religion had to become real to me, and I had to know God for myself. And I bowed over that cup of coffee. I never will forget it. . . . I prayed a prayer, and I prayed out loud that night. I said, "Lord, I'm down here trying to do what's right. I think the cause that we represent is right. But Lord, I must confess that I'm weak now. I'm faltering. I'm losing my courage. And I can't let the people see me like this because if they see me weak and losing my courage they will begin to get weak." And it seemed at that moment that I could hear an inner voice saying to me, "Martin Luther, stand up for righteousness. Stand up for justice. Stand up for truth. And lo, I will be with you, even until the end of the world." . . . I heard the voice of Jesus saying still to fight on. He promised never to leave me, never to leave me alone. No never alone. No never alone. He promised never to leave me, never to leave me alone. Almost at once my fears began to go. My uncertainty disappeared.[9]

King's kitchen table experience and Merton's Fourth and Walnut vision were breakthrough events in the lives of each man. King committed himself to the movement completely despite his growing realization—more certain as the years went by—that it would cost him his life. Merton grasped with his heart a truth that he had only known with his head: the monk left the world for the sake of the world. These events confirmed each in the path he had already started.

Both paths converged on the issue of civil rights. Merton, as well as King, perceived civil rights as a moral and religious struggle, indeed as the religious cause of the day, a view disputed by many Christians who saw it as an essentially political struggle with extremists on both sides. Merton and King had a profound sense that they and the nation were living through a *kairos*, a "time of urgent and providential election." Merton stated it plainly when he announced,

> In the Negro Christian non-violent movement, under Martin Luther King, the kairos, the "providential time," met with a courageous and enlightened response. The non-violent-Negro civil rights drive has been one of the most positive and successful expressions of Christian social action that has been seen anywhere in the twentieth century. It is certainly the greatest example of Christian faith in action in the social history of the United States.[10]

According to King, the struggle for civil rights presented the nation with an unprecedented historical opportunity. "The problem of race and color prejudice remains America's greatest moral dilemma. When one considers the impact it has on our nation, internally and externally, its resolution might well determine our destiny. History has thrust upon our generation an indescribably important task—to complete a process of democratization which our nation has too long developed too slowly."[11] But, both men warned, the moment could be lost, and if it were, the consequences would be dire. The "moment of grace," according to Merton, "will pass without effect. The merciful kairos of truth will turn into the dark hour of destruction and hate." Or as King put it, "The Negro may be God's appeal to this age—an age drifting rapidly to its doom."[12]

The concept of *kairos* gave a sense of urgency to their calls for a national renewal, a renewal that could only come about through nonviolence. For both men, nonviolence was not simply a political tactic, it was a way of life. As King outlined it, nonviolence required active resistance to evil instead of passivity; it sought to convert, not to defeat, the opponent; it was directed against evil, not against persons; it avoided internal violence, such as hatred or bitterness, as much as external violence, because hatred depersonalized the individual. Nonviolence, according to King, was based upon the belief that acceptance of suffering was redemptive, because suffering could transform both the sufferer and the oppressor; it was based upon loving others regardless of worth or merit; it was based upon the realization that all human beings are interrelated; and it was grounded in the confidence that justice would, in the end, triumph over injustice. The belief that suffering was redemptive was crucial to King as the rationale for nonviolent direct action. By accepting the violence of the oppressor, without retaliation and even without hatred, the demonstrators, he taught, could transform the oppressor's heart.[13]

Merton shared King's admiration for Gandhi and his commitment to nonviolence. In fact, Merton's first defense of Gandhian principles occurred in 1931, when as a sixteen-year-old schoolboy in England, he got into an argument with his dormitory prefect (the captain of the football team) over the legitimacy of the Mahatma's campaign to free India from British rule.[14] Gandhi's greatness, in Merton's eyes, was his profound insight into the connection between nonviolence and truth, a connection that Merton insisted was crucial if renewal of either the person or society was ever to take place. Truth, in this context, did not refer to the defense of abstract principle, still less some rigidly held ideology, but rather "the truth that is incarnate in a concrete human situation, involving living persons whose rights are denied or whose lives are threatened."[15]

Nonviolence was, in the final analysis, a way of being in the world that conformed to truth. To Merton and King alike, it was the only method of social change that took full account of the dignity of the person since it rejected the use of force and replaced coercion with an appeal to liberty and intelligence, the very qualities that constitute our humanity. Over and over again, King and Merton proclaimed the ultimate worth, the sacredness of persons. Over and over again, they lambasted current attitudes and behaviors that debased human freedom and deadened human consciousness. In particular, they condemned the mindless striving after power, status, and wealth, which we have come to call consumerism, as a dangerous collective illusion that effectively reduces persons to objects and relegates interpersonal relationship to manipulation and exploitation. In short, King warned, "we need to move from a thing-oriented society to a person-oriented society."[16] In the essay "Rain and the Rhinoceros," his most devastating critique of mass culture, Merton diagnosed consumerism as a futile attempt on our part to forget our condition of radical contingency, to suppress our awareness of the inevitability of death. Consumerism works by "creating an illusion of yourself as one who has no needs that he cannot immediately fulfill." Artificial needs are created, typically by mass media, and then "satisfied," thus holding out the spurious promise of omnipotence, but actually drawing the "consumer" into a spiraling cycle of need-gratification-need that can only lead to frustration and end in despair. Trapped in this vicious cycle, we are burdened by illusion and conditioned to "suffer all the needs that society demands we suffer."[17]

Consumerism commodifies human relationships and trivializes freedom of choice, so that individuals become alienated not only from others, but also from themselves. As Merton put it, "Our trouble is that we are alienated from our own personal reality, or true self. We do not believe in anything but money and the power or the enjoyment which come from the possession of money."[18] Alienation is the source of the disregard for persons that produces apathy, hatred, and violence. The purpose of nonviolence, then, is to oppose alienation by offering people the possibility of reconciliation, with one's self as well as with others. (This implicit critique of capitalism resembles Marx's. Both Merton and King appreciated the insights of Marxism, but rejected its atheism and its expression in totalitarian form in twentieth-century Communist regimes. Merton had flirted briefly with membership in a Communist organization during his Columbia days in the late 1930s; King had worked through Marx as part of his reading program in social philosophers of the West while doing graduate study at Boston. Independent of Marxism, both men came to the position that racism, poverty, and war are structurally related.)

The alienation of the person from himself, Merton claimed, is endemic to our society. One of the most consistent themes of his writing, as constant in his social as in his more "spiritual" books, is a distinction between the true, or inner, self and the false, or external, self. We desperately need, Merton insisted in essay after essay, to move beyond our absorption in the false self to an awareness of the true self. "To have an identity is to be awake and aware," he wrote. "But to be awake is to accept our vulnerability and death. Not out of stoicism or despair but for the sake of the invulnerable inner reality which we cannot recognize (which we can only be) but to which we awaken only when we see the un-reality of our vulnerable shell."[19] The only way to achieve this awareness is solitude, simplicity, and silence—the contemplative life. Not everyone can be a monk, but every Christian is called to develop within his or her life a dimension of silence and solitude in order to become aware of the inner self.

Moreover, Merton contended, it is crucial to come to an aware-ness of the true self in order to come to an awareness of God. As he explained:

> If we are involved only in our surface existence, in externals, and in the trivial concerns of our ego, we are untrue to Him and to our-selves. To reach a true awareness of Him as well as ourselves, we have to renounce our selfish and limited self and enter into a whole new kind of existence, discovering an inner center of motivation and love which makes us see ourselves and everything else in an entirely new light. . . . The real sense of our own existence, which is normally veiled and distorted by the routine distractions of an alienated life, is now revealed in a central intuition. What was lost and dispersed in the relative meaninglessness and triviality of pur-poseless behavior (living like a machine, pushed around by im-pulsions and suggestions from others) is brought together in fully integrated conscious significance.[20]

Influenced by the tradition of the Rhineland mystics John Tauler, Henry Suso, and especially Meister Eckhart, Merton came to a profound realization of the presence of God at the core of our being. He spoke of *le point vierge*, a still point, the "center of our nothingness where one meets God—and is found completely in His mercy."[21] Merton's most extended description of *le point vierge* occurs in the account of his Fourth and Walnut experience already quoted:

> At the center of our being is a point of nothingness which is un-touched by sin and by illusion, a point of pure truth, a point or spark which belongs entirely to God, which is never at our dis-posal, from which God disposes our lives, which is inaccessible to

the fantasies of our own mind or the brutalities of our own will. This little point of nothingness and of *absolute poverty* is the pure glory of God in us. It is so to speak His name written in us, as our poverty, as our indigence, as our dependence, as our sonship. It is like a pure diamond, blazing with the invisible light of heaven. It is in everybody, and if we could see it we would see these billions of points of light coming together in the face and blaze of a sun that would make all the darkness and cruelty of life vanish completely.[22]

To become aware of this point at the center requires that we confront our own contingency and death so that we might arrive, or rather, be given an intuition (an immediate apprehension) of the Reality in which our being is truly grounded—God. One must, according to Merton, face the poverty of the self and be ready to renounce "the empirical self, in the presence of death and nothingness," precisely "in order to overcome the ignorance and error that spring from the fear of 'being nothing.'" In this "desert of loneliness and emptiness the fear of death and the need for self-affirmation are seen to be illusory," and one begins to realize that the void is full and that the darkness is light. And so "in the heart of anguish are found the gifts of peace and understanding": compulsion, fear, and illusion yield to joy, spontaneity, and truth.[23]

Moreover, Merton insisted, this experience does not end merely in personal illumination and individual liberation; it also includes a profound realization of the unity that binds us all together, the "hidden ground of love." In awakening to our own true identity, we find not only ourselves, but also the world, our sisters and brothers, and Christ. "It is not a matter of exclusivism and 'purity' but of wholeness, wholeheartedness, unity and . . . equality which finds the same ground of love in everything."[24] The result, then, of contemplative silence and solitude should not be narcissistic self-absorption, but profound compassion for everyone and everything, a compassion that expresses itself in empathy and commitment.

For Merton, commitment to nonviolence was ultimately an affirmation of the sacredness of human life, and this understanding sprang from his own contemplative experience of the presence of God at the still point of each person's true self. Martin Luther King's vision of the human person, though differing in certain emphases from Merton's, brought him to remarkably similar conclusions. King claimed that the sacredness of persons was based on our identity as children of God, made in his image and so worthy of respect. "Every man is somebody," he remarked, because "he is a child of God."[25] The image of God, King explained, "is universally shared in equal portions by all." "Every human being has etched in his personality the indelible stamp of the Creator." If any person is "treated as anything less than a person of sacred worth, the image of God is abused in him and consequently and proportionately lost by those who inflict this abuse."[26]

His concept of the person as image of God takes on much deeper resonance when we recall that King the personalist philosopher, as well as King the Baptist minister, had worked out for himself a philosophical position in which personality, finite and infinite, was regarded as the ultimate reality of the universe. So that God, who was in Tillich's phrase the "ground of all being," was not to be viewed as merely impersonal force, but as a volitional consciousness concerned about human beings and involved in human history.

If the key concept for Merton's analysis of the person is *le point vierge*, the key theme for King's philosophy of person is *agapē*. King defined *agapē*, as distinct from *eros* and *philia*—romantic love and friendly affection—as "an understanding, redeeming good will for all men":

> It is an overflowing love which is purely spontaneous, unmotivated, groundless, and creative. It is not set in motion by any quality or function of its object. It is the love of God operating in the human heart. Agape is disinterested love. It is a love in which the individ-

ual seeks not his own good, but the good of his neighbor. . . . Agape does not begin by discriminating between worthy and unworthy people, or any qualities people possess. It begins by loving others for their sakes. It is an entirely "neighbor-regarding concern for others," which discovers the neighbor in every man it meets. . . . It springs from the need of the person—his need for belonging to the best in the human family.[27]

King depicted *agapē* as the overspill of God's love within humans. An even more striking image is his vision of love "standing at the center of the cosmos," the supreme unifying principle of life. When we love, in the sense of *agapē*, we open the "door which leads to ultimate reality."[28] In King's thought *agapē* takes on the force of a cosmic principle, a law of life, to which human behavior and human personality should conform. Thus not only acts of violence, but internal attitudes, such as hate or bitterness, even resentment, had to be abandoned because they contradicted the internal logic of personality and the ordering law of the universe.

Just as Merton taught that the experience of *le point vierge* included recognition of the unity of all persons under the aspect of being, so King taught that the experience of *agapē* revealed the mutual interrelatedness of all persons under the aegis of love. Though Merton does speak of the "ground of love," his primary emphasis is on being as the unifying principle of reality, and though King does speak of being, his main stress is on *agapē* as the principle of wholeness in the universe. This difference in emphasis—love on the one hand and being on the other—reflected two different paths taken by two different men. Contemplative solitude led Merton to a powerful experience of God's presence as Being. A life of incredible activism in the cause of social justice led King to experience the personal intervention of a God of love who promised always to sustain him. These differences stem in part from the different religious traditions that shaped the two men—in Merton's case, Western mysticism, supplemented by Eastern spirituality, especially Zen; in King's case, the social engagement of black Evangelical piety.

One can't help but speculate about other, more psychological, sources. As the son of two artists, Merton's artistic temperament and literary vocation were formed early. Writing impelled him to capture the pattern within the details, the order behind the chaos, the general beneath the particular. His focus as a writer was his own experience, but the very act of writing for publication posited the universality of that experience as a topic of significance for others. Moreover, Merton experienced early in his monastic career a great deal of ambivalence about his writing. Why should one who had left the world in search of obscurity and solitude continue to claim the world's attention so insistently by publishing book after book? Illustrating this apparent inconsistency in Merton's personality, a friend commented after his death that he was after all a "gregarious hermit." Solitude and social concern, silence and volubility, the particular and the universal, all these oppositions coincided in the transcendent experience of reality as Being in which everything connects.

Similarly, King's activism owed something to the high expectations placed upon a precocious son by a proudly self-made and highly successful father. Great expectations can be a strong motivation for achievement, and at the same time a heavy burden to carry. It is interesting that King should come to emphasize so strongly the centrality of unmerited love, the experience of being totally accepted not for one's achievement, but simply and completely for one's self.

Different emphasis and different backgrounds aside, the social vision of King, the activist, and Merton, the contemplative, converged in their mutual realization of the interrelatedness of human beings—the hidden wholeness that binds us all together. In King's words, "Whether we call it an unconscious process, an impersonal Brahman, or a Personal Being of matchless power and infinite love, there is a creative force in this universe that works to bring the disconnected aspects of reality into a harmonious whole."[29] And, in one of those eloquent formulas that he repeated in speech after speech until it became a refrain: "All life is interrelated. All men are caught in an inescapable network of mutuality, tied in a single garment of destiny."[30]

Belief in our fundamental interrelatedness moved King and Merton to take a universalist perspective on the social problems of our era. They perceived clearly, for example, the connection between the struggle for civil rights in America and the independence struggles of colonized peoples around the world. Earlier than most, they pointed out the link between violence at home and violence abroad, as they insisted upon speaking out against what Merton called an overwhelming atrocity, the Vietnam War.

Recognition of the interrelatedness of all persons, they claimed, lays upon all people of goodwill the radical obligation of compassion. Beyond barriers of race, nationality, and religion, we must identify ourselves with the poor, the oppressed, the wretched of the earth. It is our calling to become the voice of the voiceless, the face of the faceless, to an unheeding and uncaring society. Ultimately, according to King and Merton, there are no aliens, no enemies, no others, but only sisters and brothers. However, this kind of identification, if it is to be authentic instead of merely sentimental, requires suffering. Love in reality, unlike love in dreams, is a harsh and dreadful thing (as Father Zossima and Dorothy Day remind us). Compassion requires *kenōsis*, self-emptying sacrifice. *Kenōsis* might take the shape of solitude and silence as it did for Merton—the lonely self-emptying experience of nothingness that opens out into frightening darkness. Or *kenōsis* might take the form of altruistic activism, as it did for King—the daily burden of exhausting dedication to the schedules, needs, and demands of others. In either case, the cross must be borne. Compassion demands it. As both men knew well, the pattern had been set long ago by the person they tried to follow: "Though he was in the form of God, he did not deem equality with God a thing to be grasped, but emptied himself, taking the form of a slave, being born in the likeness of men. And being found in human form he humbled himself, and became obedient unto death, even death on a cross" (Phil. 2:6–8).

In the end, Merton's path and King's met at the symbol of reconciliation and compassion—the cross. Their lives bore complementary witness to the profound meditation of an earlier disciple upon that same cross: "We know what love is by this: that he laid down his life for us so that we ought to lay down our lives for others. But whoever possesses this world's goods and notices his brother in need and shuts his heart against him, how can the love of God remain in him? Dear children, let us put our love not into words or into talk but into deeds" (1 John 3:16–18).

Epilogue

A Fire in the Bones

HEADING FOR THE LIBRARY LATE ONE SUMMER afternoon
more than thirty years ago, when I was a student at Loyola University (now Loyola Marymount) in Los Angeles, I noticed a tall
Jesuit walking toward me. At the same moment, we both glanced
up. Our eyes met, and I nodded a "Good afternoon, Father."
"Good afternoon," he responded as we passed. I suddenly realized
I had just greeted John Courtney Murray. I had seen his picture
on the cover of *Time*. I had struggled through part of his celebrated and demanding book *We Hold These Truths*. I was impressed that day by his stately bearing, the liveliness of his eyes,
and most of all by the fact that this brilliant intellectual, walking
slowly across campus in the late afternoon light, was saying the
rosary.

FIRE IN THE BONES

The old meeting house caught on fire. The spirit was there. Every
heart was beating in unison as we turned our minds to God to tell
him of our sorrows here below. God saw our need and came to us.
I used to wonder what made people shout, but now I don't. There
is a joy on the inside, and it wells up so strong that we can't keep
still. It is fire in the bones. Any time that fire touches a man, he will
jump.[1]

These are the words of a former slave, describing the religious services of his people just after Emancipation. I was first arrested by these words twenty-five years ago, when I began to research and write about the religious history of African-Americans. The paradoxical conjunction of "sorrows here below" and "joy welling up on the inside" puzzled me. Over the years, the image of "fire in the bones" stuck in my memory and eventually became for me a metaphor of the distinctive character of African-American Christianity, a mood of joyful sorrow, sorrowful joy, or more accurately, sorrow merging into joy. The paradox resonated within me, stirring memories of forgotten ancestors whose stories I needed to learn, stories with important lessons not only for me, but for others as well.

What does this "fire in the bones" have to do with John Courtney Murray? One of the central concerns of Murray's intellectual life was the problem of pluralism: What truths do we Americans hold in common? Upon what basic principles can our nation, made up of people of diverse religious and moral values, reach consensus? In the essays published in that book I found so difficult in my freshman year of college, *We Hold These Truths: Catholic Reflections on the American Proposition* (1960), Murray elegantly argued that such a set of principles, a "tradition of rational truth," could be derived from natural law. Taking up Murray's interest in the question of pluralism, an issue even more hotly debated now than in his day, I would like to reflect upon the truths we hold in common from the perspective of African-American Christians, a people excluded for much of their history from full participation in their nation and their church because of race.

The issue of race did not figure in Murray's discussion of American pluralism, nor did he take sufficient account, I think, of the symbolic value of history to bind a people together (or conversely, to keep them apart). Beyond allegiance to a set of shared principles, a prime source of identity for a nation is history, construed as a set of interlocking stories that we tell one another about our origins and our past. I mean the mythic history that establishes our sense of national identity, destiny, and purpose (Lincoln's "mystic chords of memory"). It is important to note that our sense of common history can change over time to accommodate our expanding awareness of the variety of who we are ethnically, racially, and religiously. The expansion of our historical vision usually occurs in response to social pressure from some group whose story has been left out of the national story. This was precisely the impetus for the black studies movement of the late 1960s and early 1970s, the period when I came to intellectual and academic maturity. That cultural movement—mirroring the social and political movement to guarantee civil rights for blacks—effectively demonstrated that African-Americans, despite their absence from the dominant academic and popular versions of American history, had been of central importance to the development of the nation. Moreover, the neglect of black history not only distorted American history, but distorted both white and black Americans' perceptions of who they were. For a people to "lose" their history, to have their story denigrated as insignificant, is a devastating blow, an exclusion tantamount to denying their full humanity. To ignore the history of another people whose fate has been intimately bound up with your own is to forgo self-understanding. Thus for many of us, the attempt to recover African-American history had more than academic significance. I felt that in the recovery of this history lay the restoration of my past, my self, my people.

I was born in 1943, during the second war in this century to rack the world with death and destruction and untold misery—a war that demonstrated the horrors that doctrines of racial supremacy can effect. I was born into a country and a part of the country burdened by racism and racial oppression. I was born black in the American South, in the state of Mississippi. I was born into a family of Indian, French, German, and African ancestry in a small town on the Gulf

of Mexico named after a king of France, Bay St. Louis. I was born
three months after my father was shot and killed by another man, a
white man, in Mississippi, in 1943.

Intending to help develop a new African-American historiography, I chose to write a history of the religious life of slaves in the United States. As I sought sources for my study, I became fascinated by the voices of former slaves preserved in narrative accounts of their lives under slavery, not just as historical evidence but as voices that seemed to be speaking directly to me. These voices were special: they rang with the authenticity that comes from those who have endured brutal suffering and triumphed over it. In my historical writing, I tried to capture the tenor of these voices, their rhythms, and especially the wisdom that they conveyed.

What did they say, these voices of elderly black Americans, who had lived part of their lives under slavery, and all their lives under discrimination? They spoke of slavery as a central religious and moral fact in the history of our nation, a fact that could not be excused as an exception to the "real" American story. Their voices contradicted the proposition that America is the story of the gradual expansion of freedom and opportunity to a wider and wider group of people. The national story has to include the ongoing rejection and degradation of others because of race. Those versions of the American story, therefore, that tend to be triumphalistic, smug, or celebratory fail the truth. What's more, they are dangerous because they facilitate our tendency to ignore the terrible urgency of those who still live in the long shadow of the plantation, trapped in poverty and despair. The moral claim laid upon us by their ancestors' insistent voices is continual awareness that racial inequity has been woven into the fabric of our society from the start and is still very much a part of its social and economic pattern.

I was born into a family that was Roman Catholic as far back as we knew. I was baptized in St. Rose de Lima, a black church, and given the name Albert Jordy, after my dead father. When I was two, my mother, my sisters, and I moved to the North, partly because of what had happened to my father. But we returned during summers to visit relatives down home. One summer down South I remember especially well; I remember one Sunday when we had missed Mass at St. Rose, so we went to the white church, Our Lady of the Gulf. We sat in back, I remember, squeezed together in a half pew. I remember going to receive Holy Communion. I remember the priest carrying the host; I remember him passing me by, and again passing me by, carrying the host in his hands, passing me by until he had given communion to all the white people; I remember, I was seven years old.

As I continued to teach and to write about the religious history of African-Americans, I encountered time and again the charge that Christianity, as a compensatory and otherworldly religion, distracted black people from their situation and encouraged them to accept their lot as the will of God. "Take this world but give me Jesus." On the contrary, the voices I heard spoke, in the main, with righteous anger and prophetic certainty about the destruction awaiting this nation unless it repented the evil of racism. Their God was a God of justice, they asserted, the Lord of history, who intervened in human affairs to cast down the mighty and uplift the lowly. And a whole cloud of biblical witnesses supported their case: the children of Israel freed from Egyptian bondage, Daniel standing unscathed in the lions' den, Shadrach, Meshach, and Abednego safe in the fiery furnace, and so on and on down the litany of prophets, apostles, and martyrs whose lineage they claimed as their own. Slavery and racial exclusion contradicted the essence of Christianity. "Bear ye one another's burdens. How can the master claim to bear my burdens, when he burdens me down with the heavy chains of oppression?" demanded a group of slaves in 1774.[2] Any form of Christianity that condones slavery or racial discrimination is to that extent false and will be punished. "Ain't everybody talking 'bout heaven, gonna go to heaven." Slaveholding and segregating Christians practiced a perversion of Christianity. The segregation of black and white churches signified the existence of two Christianities in this nation, and the deep chasm that divided them demonstrated the failure of the nation's predominant religious institution, the major source of its common symbols, images, and values, to achieve meaningful, sustained community across racial lines.

In my hometown there was a Roman Catholic seminary. It was founded in 1920 to train black men to be priests, because most other seminaries would not accept them. It was named for St. Augustine, since he was from Africa. My stepfather studied there. He was ordained a priest, but in 1947 he left. He left disillusioned and angry because of the racial prejudice he encountered in the church, even among fellow priests. Years later he would still rage when he remembered the wrongs done to him and to other black priests. Ad introibo ad altare Dei, ad Deum qui laetificat juventutem meum. When I was ten I became an altar boy. The sound of Latin, the glow of candles, the fragrance of incense, the splendor of the altar, the solemnity of the saints' statues surrounded me with sacred mystery. May processions, benedictions, daily school masses, music, chants, the liturgical seasons, the sacraments, all supported within me a profound sense of the tangible presence of God. Despite my stepfather's experience, and my own, of racism in the church, I believed, as did he, that the sacraments worked (ex opere operato). From the age of ten, I wanted to be a priest. I wanted to stand at the altar and offer God in my hands.

So it was that when I came to investigate the religions that enslaved Africans brought to the Americas, I encountered something that seemed very familiar, a correspondence that Africans themselves had discovered centuries ago between their religions and Roman Catholic Christianity. The most obvious of these correspondences was the identification of Catholic saints with African spirits, so characteristic of African-American religions like Voodoo and Santería. Though my family has Louisiana roots, none of us, as far as I know, served the *lwa* (practiced Voodoo). No, African religions seemed familiar because they shared with Catholicism a sacramental vision of the world in which another world, a spiritual world, coinheres with this one. Behind its flat surface, our day-to-day world opens onto depths full of meaning, pattern, and spiritual presence. Ritual, like a doorway, gives access to this spiritual world. Through ritual we step into a kingdom of divine light, mystery, and wonder. The material objects of ritual not only symbolize spiritual realities, but make them present: incense becomes the fragrance of prayer; the light of the candles becomes the flame of devotion; the images of the saints enable the power of ancestors to help the living. Liturgical ritual in African religions, as well as Catholicism, culminates in moments of transparency between the worlds when the divine and the human touch and life is transformed. From this perspective, our society, in general, seems ritually and symbolically impoverished. (The national civic symbols and rituals that do exist are weak and shallow sources of identity and community.) Societies need ritual to transmit meaning and value from one generation to another. Without effective and affective shared rituals, our sense of community atrophies. We are left with the symbols manufactured by mass culture for ceremonies of common consumption.

There were correspondences that obtained between African religions and Protestantism as well, though more subtle than those associated with Catholicism. In the emotional preaching and ecstatic behavior of Baptist and Methodist revival services, African-American slaves encountered a ritual equivalent to the spirit possession ceremonies of Africa. The crucial factor linking the two traditions was a conviction that authentic worship required an observable experience of the divine presence. "It ain't enough to talk about God, you've got to feel Him moving on the altar of your heart," as one former slave explained.[3] Ritual, in this liturgical perspective, is supposed to bring the divine tangibly into this world. The presence of God becomes manifest in the words, the gestures, and the bodies of the believers. Their praying, singing, preaching, and dancing occasion as well as signal the Spirit's arrival. In this form of African and African-American ritual, the divine is embodied in the faithful. The emotional ecstasy of black Protestant worship symbolizes a profound religious truth: the preeminent place of God's presence in this world is the person. His altar is the human heart. Moreover, it is the whole person, body as well as spirit, that makes God present. In a society chronically split between body and spirit, African-American ritual exemplifies embodied spirit and inspirited body in gesture, dance, song, and performed word. In worship the human becomes an icon of God. A radically personal vision of life flows from this liturgical sensibility. Contrary to the depersonalizing pressures of slavery and racial oppression, the person is of ultimate value as image of the divine. Anything, then, that defaces that image is sacriligious.

As I wrote and taught about African religions, their transmission and transformation in America, I realized that they represented a legacy of wisdom about the nature of the world and people in the world from which we all could benefit. Contemporary perspectives might be complemented and enhanced by the traditions of these ancient societies, unknown to most of us. For example, in the personalized world of traditional African religion, the self is conceived as relational. Each person is constituted by a web of interpersonal relationships. Our health, our fortunes, our very lives depend upon the state of our relationships with others, including those who have gone before, our ancestors, who continue to figure prominently in the progress of our lives. By contrast, the tendency of American culture to overemphasize the individualized self empties life of the communal presence that gives depth and background to our existence. Similarly, a greater appreciation of the self as relational might help us perceive the selfish desire for aggrandizement hiding behind many of our images of success. To achieve at the expense of others, from the perspective of traditional African religions, is witchcraft, pure and simple. And if you choose to move too far outside or too far above your community, you risk becoming bewitched.

In Bay St. Louis, unlike the North, there always seemed to be time and space enough for the long-time love. In the evening twilight, we gathered for supper. The table was heavy with food, laughter, and stories, stories about the old people that went on long into the night, until the last warm sweet sip of anisette placed a benediction on the evening. I heard stories about my great-grandmother, who'd been a slave. She had to flee New Orleans with her son, my grandfather, because his father, a merchant mariner, wanted to take the boy with him when he returned to Germany. They remembered my great-grandmother starching and ironing white shirtwaists while singing snatches of opera she had heard in New Orleans. Her grandchildren used to laugh behind her back and call her "Black Patty" after the famous Fisk Jubilee singer. There was no rush about them, as with the people up North. They attended carefully to the daily tasks of community. Graciousness with others, gentleness, generosity, care, kindness, politeness—these were the virtues of down home. Being known, because my grandparents were known, I glimpsed the deep patterns of my people, patterns that healed. These were my people. They had an ease about them that put others at ease, like a warm embrace. Up North, black Catholics were few. I was one of a handful of black students in St. Thomas school. I didn't say it, but I felt different, alone, far from my people, far from home.

A peculiar people, Americans have always thought of themselves as a chosen people, specially blessed by God with freedom, liberty, and prosperity. At best, this national myth of chosenness has supported ideals of service, tolerance, and freedom; at worst, attitudes of chauvinism, materialism, and militarism. African-American Christianity has continuously confronted the nation with troubling questions about the myth of choseness. After all, if Americans are the New Israel, and America the Promised Land, what are we to make of the perennial claims of black Christians that they are the children of Israel, at last freed from slavery, but still far from crossing into the Promised Land? Election, moreover, brings not only preeminence, elevation, and glory, but as black Christians knew all too well, humiliation, suffering, and rejection. Chosenness, as reflected in the life of Jesus, led to a cross. The lives of his disciples have been signed with that cross. To be chosen, in this perspective, means joining company not with the powerful, but with those who suffer, the outcast, the poor. Being chosen means entering the mystery of suffering in the sure hope of coming through to the other side.

African-American Christians believed they were a chosen people, not because they were black, nor because they suffered, but because their history fit the pattern of salvation revealed to them in the Bible. They saw themselves in Christ, the suffering servant. Their lives modeled the paradoxes of the gospel: in weakness lies strength, in loss, gain, in death, life. "Blessed are the poor, for theirs is the kingdom of heaven. Blessed are the meek, for they shall inherit the earth. Blessed are those who hunger and thirst after righteousness, for they shall be filled."

The problem of suffering was complicated for black Christians by racism. In accepting their suffering, black Christians were not accepting the racist argument that God intended them to suffer; they were asserting that chosenness empowers people to make something out of suffering. In the end, suffering is a fact of life.

We can try to ignore it, evade it, deaden it, overpower it, but only at the cost of our humanity. To recognize that life brings suffering does not mean we have to succumb to fatalism. Suffering and injustice must be challenged at the deepest existential level, the level of defeat and despair that Christ overcame through his passion, death, and resurrection. In this sense, African-American Christianity is a paradigm of the central mystery of the gospel, sorrow becomes joy, death yields life.

We should not underestimate the difficulty of living such beliefs. The temptations to despair, to reject Christianity as white man's religion, to abandon belief in a God who permits the innocent to suffer were, by all accounts, very real. Like Job, black Christians received no logical answer to the question of why they suffered, but only the command to trust in God. Like Jacob they wrestled all night and instead of achieving victory gained only a blessing. Two sources sustained them in their struggle against despair, the personal experience of conversion and the communal experience of worship. The conversion experiences of black Christians grounded their identity in the knowledge that they were accepted by God, indeed, were of ultimate value in the eyes of God, no matter what white men thought.

I travel to the low country of Georgia and the South Carolina coastal islands to talk to elderly black Christians about their experience of conversion, about a process called seeking they underwent many years ago. Led by the Spirit into the wilderness to pray, each had a spiritual father or mother to examine dreams and visions and to serve as a guide in the way of salvation. Now in their eighties and nineties, these are hard-pressed people who've been poor all their lives. They've been through the fire and refined like gold. When they speak about their conversion experiences of sixty and seventy years ago, their faces light up with joy. I ask one ninety-five-year-old man what the difference is between his time and mine. "Love," he replied. "Too much love has gone out of the world. We didn't have nothing and we helped one another. Now it seems like all everybody is interested in is making the dollar."

From black people like these came a music that constitutes one of this nation's most significant contributions to world culture. And many around the world have been moved by their songs, songs that transform the particular suffering of one people into a parable of human experience. What is the meaning in all this sorrow? What good is it? Simply this. It must be lived through; it can't be evaded by any of the subterfuges of power or spurious means of escape devised by people to distract one another from reality. Life in a minor key is life as it is, bittersweet, joyful sadness. Unless we are mature enough, realistic enough, to accept sorrow, we will never be able to truly laugh, to be genuinely creative, to authentically love. Instead, we succumb to illusion, becoming preoccupied by an ever-spiraling cycle of needs, in a vain attempt to deny suffering and death. We become bewitched by the illusion that we have no needs that we ourselves can't meet, that we are omnipotent, that we control our own lives. Illusions of power become dangerous when we try to live them out by controlling others. This deformation of our humanity takes on exceptional force because it is driven by a deep, inchoate fear. The spirituals speak of an alternative. They reveal the capability of the human spirit to transcend bitter sorrow and to resist the persistent attempts of evil to strike it down.

One Sunday, last December, at the start of a very bleak winter, I stood in the front of Saints Peter and Paul Orthodox Church to receive the sacrament of Chrismation. The priest anointed my head, eyes, nostrils, ears, lips, chest, hands, and feet with holy oil and gave me a lit candle to hold as I stood for Divine Liturgy. After the anointing I thought about the last step in the process of icon painting, which is the application of warm oil. The oil serves to bind together the colors of the icon and to bring out their depth. At the beginning of the liturgy we sing the words of Psalm 103, "Bless the Lord, O my soul and all that is within me bless his holy name." And I am moved once again by the sad joyfulness of the chant tones. Once again I feel the prayers of the congregation as if their hands hold me up. I think back to the night of Pascha when we had processed around the church with lit candles and then stood at the doors of the church chanting "Christ is risen!" When the doors opened and we all moved into the church, I felt the presence of generations of Christians standing with us, generations moving into the church with us, present with us on Pascha, our ancestors in the faith.

Our nation too has ancestors. Now, as much as ever, we stand in need of their presence. We, the American people, need to hear and to listen to the stories of all our forefathers and -mothers. We need to be informed by the memories of their lives. Can these bones live, these dry bones? If we allow them to be reknit, re-membered. Memory, story, ritual—these are all ways of re-membering a community broken by hate, rage, injustice, fear. Not to avenge, nor to make up for, not undoing what can't be undone, but perhaps to heal. There are those who fear that the stories won't cohere, that they will remain a disparate set of unrelated or conflict-ridden experiences that only confirm our feelings of divisiveness, of us against them. Perhaps. But I am convinced that if we listen, truly listen, to the stories of others, something else will happen. We will find ourselves intrigued by the drama of these stories, moved by their poignancy, and finally, surprised at the common humanity that lies beneath their distinctive details. In the end, what we hold in common is a set of shared stories. If we seek commonality, we will discover it in the telling and listening to each other's stories, confident that an adequate history of the varied races and religions who came to dwell in this land will reflect our continually expanding American identity. Because of our habitual tendency to repeat the congratulatory story, excluding others that don't fit a celebratory mood, we must resist the collective pressure to abandon, deny, or forget the particular stories of all our people and our connection to them.

I grew up without knowing the full story of my father's death. My mother and my stepfather decided not to tell me until I started college because they did not want me to grow up hating white folks. As a result, I wondered if the story were shameful—otherwise they would have told me. I never knew my father. I had no memories of him. I had no stories of him—only one blurry picture. I knew only his absence. Several months ago, I went back to Mississippi in search of my father. I didn't know what I'd find after all this time, only that I needed to go. I talked to aunts and uncles, cousins, and close family friends. I found two newspaper accounts of his death. I spoke with the son of the man who killed my father. On the last day of my trip, I went to visit my father's grave. I had been there many times before, but for the first time, I suddenly began to cry. I cried for him, for my mother, for my sisters, for a father and son who never met. Then, as if in memory, I saw him. I saw him laughing; I saw him raging; I saw him shot, and falling, falling into my arms, into my life. After all these years of waiting, my father and I have finally met. I bend down, pick up some dirt from his grave and rub it on my head. All the sorrow wells up inside me and merges with the joy of meeting him, finally for the first time . . .

It is fire in the bones.

Notes

PROLOGUE

1. Elizabeth Ware Pierson, ed. *Letters From Port Royal, 1862–1868* (Boston, 1906; New York: Arno Press, 1969), 65.

2. The term "Jesus movement" attempts to avoid an anachronistic reading of the "Church" back into the first century.

3. The term "hidden wholeness" alludes to the title of a book by John Howard Griffin about the esthetic vision of Thomas Merton. Merton wrote an insightful essay about the academic life, "Learning to Live," published in *Love and Living* (New York: Farrar, Straus, Giroux, 1979), 3–14.

4. Edmund S. Morgan, "Slavery and Freedom: The American Paradox," *Journal of American History* 59 (1972): 1–29; *American Slavery, American Freedom: The Ordeal of Colonial Virginia* (New York: W. W. Norton, 1975).

5. Gomes Eannes de Zurara, *The Chronicle of the Discovery and Conquest of Guinea,* trans. Charles R. Beazley and Edgar Prestage, 2 vols. (London: Hakluyt Society, ser. 1, vols. 95 and 100, 1896, 1899), 1:81–82, 84–85.

6. I use as a title for this section that of Dom Jean Leclercq's admirable study of monastic culture. I am convinced that the contemplative tradition has a lot to say to us who struggle with the relationship of knowledge to faith.

7. Barbara Leigh Smith Bodichon, diary entry of 12 December 1857,

in *An American Diary, 1857–1858*, ed. Joseph W. Reed, Jr. (London: Routledge and Kegan Paul, 1972), 65.

8. Rayford W. Logan, *The Negro in American Life and Thought: The Nadir, 1877–1901* (New York: Dial Press, 1954).

9. Howard Thurman, *With Hand and Heart: The Autobiography of Howard Thurman* (New York: Harcourt Brace Jovanovich, 1979), 134.

CHAPTER ONE. AFRICAN-AMERICANS, EXODUS, AND THE AMERICAN ISRAEL

1. Peter Kalm, *Travels into North America*, 2d ed.; reprinted in John Pinkerton, ed., *A General Collection of the Best and Most Interesting Voyages and Travels*, vol. 13 (London, 1812), 503.

2. Thomas Secker, Sermon before the S.P.G., 1740/1; reprinted in Frank J. Klingberg, *Anglican Humanitarianism in Colonial New York* (Philadelphia: Church Historical Association, 1940), 223.

3. Winthrop D. Jordan, *White over Black: American Attitudes toward the Negro, 1550–1812* (Baltimore: Penguin Books, 1969), 191.

4. Klingberg, *Anglican Humanitarianism*, 217.

5. David Benedict, *Fifty Years among the Baptists* (New York, 1860), 93–94.

6. Charles F. James, ed., *Documentary History of the Struggle for Religious Liberty in Virginia* (Lynchburg, Va., 1900), 84–85.

7. Donald G. Mathews, *Slavery and Methodism: A Chapter in American Morality, 1780–1845* (Princeton, 1965), 293–99; Robert B. Semple, *A History of the Rise and Progress of the Baptists in Virginia*, ed. George W. Beale (Philadelphia, 1894), 105.

8. Wesley M. Gewehr, *The Great Awakening in Virginia, 1740–1790* (Durham, N.C., 1930), 244–48.

9. Ibid., 240–41.

10. Semple, *Baptists in Virginia*, 59.

11. George P. Rawick, ed., *The American Slave: A Composite Autobiog-*

raphy, vol. 8, *Arkansas Narratives* (Westport, Conn: Greenwood Press, 1972), pt. 1, 35.

12. A. M. Chreitzberg, *Early Methodism in the Carolinas* (Nashville, 1897), 158–59.

13. A. M. French, *Slavery in South Carolina and the Ex-Slaves; or, The Port Royal Mission* (New York, 1862), 127.

14. Reprinted in Conrad Cherry, ed., *God's New Israel: Religious Interpretations of American Destiny* (Englewood Cliffs, N.J.: Prentice-Hall, 1971), 43.

15. Reprinted in ibid., 83–84.

16. Ibid., 66.

17. Maria W. Stewart, *Religion and the Pure Principles of Morality, the Sure Foundation On Which We Must Build* (Boston, 1831); reprinted in Marilyn Richardson, ed., *Maria W. Stewart, America's First Black Woman Political Writer: Essays and Speeches* (Bloomington: Indiana University Press, 1987), 39.

18. Mary A. Livermore, *My Story of the War* (Hartford, Conn., 1889), 260–61.

19. W. G. Kephart, letter of May 9, 1864, Decatur, Ala., American Missionary Association Archives, Amistad Research Center, Tulane University, New Orleans.

20. W. Paul Quinn, *The Sword of Truth Going "Forth Conquering and to Conquer . . ."* (1834); reprinted in Dorothy Porter, ed., *Early Negro Writing, 1760–1837* (Boston: Beacon Press, 1971), 635.

21. Frederick Douglass, *The Life and Times of Frederick Douglass*, rev. ed. (1892; reprint, London: Collier-Macmillan, 1962), 159–60.

22. *American Missionary* 6, no. 2 (February 1862): 33.

23. Norman R. Yetman, ed., *Voices from Slavery* (New York: Holt, Rinehart and Winston, 1970), 75.

24. Sermon of April 3, 1968, delivered at Mason Temple, Memphis,

Tennessee; reprinted in James M. Washington, ed., *A Testament of Hope: The Essential Writings and Speeches of Martin Luther King, Jr.* (San Francisco: Harper and Row, 1986), p. 286.

CHAPTER TWO. "ETHIOPIA SHALL SOON STRETCH FORTH HER HANDS"

1. Francis, J. Grimke, *The Works of Francis J. Grimke*, ed. Carter G. Woodson, 4 vols. (Washington, D.C.: Associated Publishers, 1942), 1:291.

2. Arthur F. Raper, *The Tragedy of Lynching* (Montclair, N.J.: Patterson, Smith, 1969), 480. The *Richmond Planet* to which Grimke refers kept a month-by-month total of lynchings during the 1890s (Grimke, *Works*, 1:296-97).

3. Grimke, *Works*, 1:268.

4. Ibid., 267.

5. Ibid., vii-xxii, 268.

6. Gerda Lerner, *The Grimke Sisters from South Carolina: Rebels against Slavery* (Boston: Houghton Mifflin, 1967), 358-66.

7. Grimke, *Works*, 1:269-70.

8. See Lawrence W. Levine, *Black Culture and Black Consciousness: Afro-American Folk Thought from Slavery to Freedom* (New York: Oxford University Press, 1977), 33-55; Albert J. Raboteau, *Slave Religion: The "Invisible Institution" in the Antebellum South* (New York: Oxford University Press, 1978), 243-64.

9. William Miller, *A Sermon on the Abolition of the Slave Trade: Delivered in the African Church, New York, on the First of January, 1810* (New York, 1810), 4; William T. Alexander, *History of the Colored Race in America* (1887; reprint, New York: Negro Universities Press, 1968), 8; Hosea Easton, *A Treatise on the Intellectual Character, and Civil and Political Condition of the Colored People of the United States* (Boston, 1837), 9-10.

10. William Wells Brown, *The Black Man: His Antecedents, His Genius, and His Achievements* (Boston, 1863), 32; Miller, *On the Abolition of the*

Slave Trade, 5–6; George Washington Williams, *History of the Negro Race in America*, 2 vols. (New York, 1883), 1:109; Easton, *A Treatise*, 19–20.

11. Absalom Jones, *A Thanksgiving Sermon Preached January 1, 1808, in St. Thomas's, or the African Episcopal Church, Philadelphia: An Account of the Abolition of the African Slave Trade* (Philadelphia, 1808), 18; Miller, *On the Abolition of the Slave Trade*, 7–8; Williams, *History of the Negro Race* 1:113–14.

12. Nathaniel Paul, *An Address, Delivered on the Celebration of the Abolition of Slavery in New York, July 5, 1827* (Albany, 1827), 10–11.

13. See the sermons of Jones, Miller, and Paul. The anniversaries of these occasions were observed down to Emancipation.

14. Leonard I. Sweet, *Black Images of America, 1784–1870* (New York: W. W. Norton, 1976), 35–68.

15. John H. Bracey, Jr., August Meier, and Elliott Rudwick, eds. *Black Nationalism in America* (Indianapolis: Bobbs-Merrill, 1970), 38–48. See Martin R. Delany, *The Condition, Elevation, Emigration, and Destiny of the Colored People of the United States, Politically Considered* (Philadelphia, 1852); and *Official Report of the Niger Valley Exploring Party* (New York, 1861); Henry McNeal Turner, "Essay: The American Negro and the Fatherland," in *Africa and the American Negro: Addresses and Proceedings of the Congress on Africa*, ed. J. W. E. Bowen (Atlanta, 1896), 195–98; see also Turner's writings and speeches collected in Edwin S. Redkey, ed., *Respect Black* (New York: Arno Press, 1971).

16. Daniel Coker, quoted in Bracey, Meier, and Rudwick, *Black Nationalism*, 46–47.

17. George B. Peabody, "The Hope of Africa," *AME Church Review*, 7, no. 1 (July 1890): 58–59. Peabody was identified as an African studying at Lincoln University!

18. Alexander Crummell, *Christian Recorder*, September 23, 1865; "The Obligation of American Black Men for the Redemption of Africa," *African Repository* 48, no. 6 (June 1872): 162–68; *The Future of Africa* (New York, 1862); *Africa and America* (Springfield, Mass., 1891).

19. Emmanuel K. Love, Baptist Foreign Mission Convention Minutes,

1889, 7–8, cited in James M. Washington, "The Origins and Emergence of Black Baptist Separatism, 1863–1897" (Ph.D. dissertation, Yale University, 1979), 159; J. Sella Martin, "A Speech before the Paris Anti-Slavery Conference, August 27 1867," reprinted in Carter G. Woodson, ed., *Negro Orators* (Washington, D.C.: Associated Publishers, 1925), 261; Edward W. Blyden, "The African Problem and the Method of Its Solution," *AME Church Review* 7, no. 2 (October 1890): 205, 213. See St. Claire Drake, *The Redemption of Africa and Black Religion* (Chicago: Third World Press, 1970).

20. T. Thomas Fortune, *Black and White: Land, Labor, and Politics in the South* (1884; reprint, Chicago: Johnson Publishing, 1970), 86–87.

21. Williams, *History of the Negro Race*, 1:114; Edward W. Blyden, *Liberia's Offering* (New York, 1862), 82–83; Easton, *A Treatise*, 20.

22. Peter Gilbert, ed., *Selected Writings of John Edward Bruce: Militant Black Journalist* (New York: Arno Press, 1971), 49.

23. David Walker, *Appeal to the Coloured Citizens of the World*, 3d ed. (Boston, 1830); reprinted in Herbert Aptheker, ed., *One Continual Cry* (New York: Humanities Press, 1965), 104.

24. *Minutes and Proceedings of the First Annual Convention of the People of Colour . . .* (Philadelphia, 1831), 10–11; *Christian Recorder*, July 15, 1865. See also Frederick Douglass, "Fifth of July Speech, Rochester, N.Y., 1852," frequently reprinted.

25. Levi J. Coppin, editorial, *AME Church Review* 7, no. 1 (July 1890): 102–3; Walker, *Appeal to the Colored Citizens*, 81 n; *Minutes of the Fourth Annual Convention for the Improvement of the Free People of Colour . . . New York, June 2–12, 1834* (New York, 1834), 27–30; James Porter, "Afro-American Methodism as a Factor in the Progress of Our Race," *AME Church Review* 7, no. 3 (January 1891): 321; *Minutes and Proceedings of the First Annual Meeting of the American Reform Society* (Philadelphia, 1837), reprinted in Dorothy Porter, ed., *Early Negro Writing, 1760–1837* (Boston: Beacon Press, 1971), 203.

26. T. G. Steward, *The End of the World; Or, Clearing the Way for the Fullness of the Gentiles* (Philadelphia, 1888), 119, 127.

27. James Theodore Holly, "The Divine Plan of Human Redemption,

In Its Ethnological Development," *AME Church Review* 1 (October 1884): 79–85. For an interesting analysis of the idea of blacks as a messianic people, see Wilson Jeremiah Moses, *Black Messiahs and Uncle Toms: Social and Literary Manipulations of a Religious Myth* (University Park: Pennsylvania State University Press, 1982).

CHAPTER THREE. "HOW FAR THE PROMISED LAND?"

1. Martin Luther King, Jr., *Stride toward Freedom: The Montgomery Story* (New York: Harper and Row, 1958), 70.

2. Appeal to Governor Thomas Gage and the Massachusetts General Court, May 25, 1774, *Collections of the Massachusetts Historical Society*, 5th ser., 3 (1877):432–33.

3. David Walker, *Appeal to the Coloured Citizens of the World*, 3d ed. (Boston, 1830); reprinted in Herbert Aptheker, ed., *One Continual Cry* (New York: Humanities Press, 1965), 13–14.

4. King read Ramsey's *Basic Christian Ethics* and Nygren's *Agape and Ethics* in a course on Christianity and society in the spring of 1951, his last year at Crozier. Whole sentences and paragraphs of *Stride toward Freedom* would be taken from Ramsey and Nygren without acknowledgment. See David J. Garrow, *Bearing the Cross: Martin Luther King, Jr., and the Southern Christian Leadership Conference* (New York: William Morrow, 1986), 112. See chapter 9 for more detailed discussion of King's developing philosophy.

5. King, *Stride toward Freedom*, 101.

6. Ibid., 61.

7. Martin Luther King, Jr., "Letter from Birmingham Jail," in *Why We Can't Wait* (New York: New American Library, 1963), 92–93.

8. King, *Stride toward Freedom*, 62.

9. Ibid., 63, 224.

10. Ibid., 224.

11. Ibid., 86. "Letter from Birmingham Jail," dated April 16, 1963, was first published as a pamphlet by the American Friends Committee and then appeared in *Why We Can't Wait* (1963). It has been frequently

reprinted. "Paul's Letter to the American Christians" was preached by King in 1955 as a radio sermon and was published in Martin Luther King, Jr., *Strength to Love* (Cleveland: Collins and World, 1977; reprint, Philadelphia: Fortress Press, 1981).

12. King, *"Letter from Birmingham Jail,"* 77.

13. *Stride toward Freedom*, 191.

14. Reprinted in James M. Washington, ed., *A Testament of Hope: The Essential Writings and Speeches of Martin Luther King, Jr.* (San Francisco: Harper and Row, 1968), 231–44.

15. Ibid., 237.

CHAPTER FOUR. RICHARD ALLEN AND THE
AFRICAN CHURCH MOVEMENT

1. Richard Allen, *The Life Experience and Gospel Labors of the Rt. Rev. Richard Allen* (Nashville: Abingdon Press, 1960; Bicentennial edition, 1983), 24.

2. See Charles H. Wesley, *Richard Allen: Apostle of Freedom* (Washington, D.C.: Associated Publishers, 1935); Carol V. R. George, *Segregated Sabbaths: Richard Allen and the Emergence of Independent Black Churches, 1760–1840* (New York: Oxford University Press, 1973); Milton C. Sernett, *Black Religion and American Evangelicalism* (Metuchen, N.J.: Scarecrow Press, 1975); and Gary B. Nash, *Forging Freedom: The Formation of Philadelphia's Black Community, 1720–1840* (Cambridge: Harvard University Press, 1988).

3. Allen, *Life Experience*, 15–16.

4. Gary Nash, "New Light on Richard Allen: The Early Years of Freedom, *William and Mary Quarterly*, 3d ser., 46, no. 2 (April 1989): 339.

5. Allen, *Life Experience*, 24; "Preamble of the Articles of Association of the Free African Society" (1778), reprinted in William Douglass, *Annals of the First African Church in the United States of America, now styled The African Episcopal Church of St. Thomas* (Philadelphia, 1862), 15.

6. Douglass, *Annals*, 23 n.

7. Benjamin Rush to Granville Sharp, August 1791, in *Letters of Ben-*

jamin Rush, 2 vols., ed. L. H. Butterfield (Princeton: Princeton University Press, 1951), 1: 608.

8. Quoted in Wesley, *Richard Allen*, 89.

9. Allen, *Life Experience*, 29–30.

10. The "African Supplement" was appended to Allen's autobiography (*Life Experience*, 37–41).

11. Ibid., 35.

12. *The Doctrines and Discipline of the African Methodist Episcopal Church*, 1st ed. (Philadelphia, 1817), 14.

13. The pamphlet by Tudas, *Facts Relative to the Government of the African Methodist Episcopal Church Called Bethel* has not been found. The *Sword of Truth* was published in Philadelphia in 1823.

14. Allen, *Life Experience*, 23.

15. Ibid., 73.

16. Ibid., 69.

17. *An Address to Those Who Keep Slaves and Approve the Practice* was appended to Allen's autobiography (*Life Experience*, 69–71).

18. *Minutes and Proceedings of the First Annual Convention of the People of Colour* . . . (Philadelphia, 1831); reprinted in Dorothy Porter, ed., *Early Negro Writing, 1760–1837* (Boston: Beacon Press, 1971), 179–81.

CHAPTER FIVE. THE BLACK CHURCH

1. Although historical study of the effects of migration and urbanization upon the black church has tended to focus exclusively on the movement of rural black southerners to the North, significant urbanization of blacks occurred in the South and the West. In the past decade, moreover, a sizable black migration has gone from North to South. See Harry A. Ploski and Ernest Kaiser, *The Negro Almanac* (New York: Bellwether, 1971), 343–67; William C. Matney and Dwight L. Johnson, *America's Black Population 1970 to 1982: A Statistical View* (Washington, D.C.: U.S. Bureau of the Census, 1983).

2. Louise Venable Kennedy, *The Negro Peasant Turns Cityward: Effects of Recent Migrations to Northern Centers* (New York: Columbia University Press, 1930), 202–6; Carter G. Woodson, *History of the Negro Church* (1921, reprint, Washington, D.C.: Associated Publishers, 1972), 252–60; Henry Hugh Proctor, *Between Black and White: Autobiographical Sketches* (Boston: Pilgrim Press, 1925), 106–8; William M. Welty, "Black Shepherds: A Study of the Leading Negro Clergymen in New York City, 1900–1940" (Ph.D. diss., New York University, 1969), 283–85.

3. St. Clair Drake and Horace R. Cayton, *Black Metropolis: A Study of Negro Life in a Northern City* (New York: Harcourt, Brace, 1945), 632–36; Benjamin E. Mays and Joseph W. Nicholson, *The Negro's Church* (1933; reprint, New York: Russell and Russell, 1969), 198–229.

4. Drake and Cayton, *Black Metropolis*, 641–46; Arthur Huff Fauset, *Black Gods of the Metropolis: Negro Religious Cults in the Urban North* (1944; reprint, Philadelphia: University of Pennsylvania Press, 1971); George Shuster and Robert M. Kearns, *Statistical Profile of Black Catholics* (Washington, D.C.: Josephite Pastoral Center, 1976), 34.

5. Robert Farris Thompson, *Flash of the Spirit: African and Afro-American Art and Philosophy* (New York: Random House, 1983), 3–97; Carl M. Hunt, *Oyotunji Village. The Yoruba Movement in America* (Washington, D.C.: University Press of America, 1979).

6. Drake and Cayton organized their discussion of urban black religion around class distinctions, but their own evidence suggests that the situation was more complex (see *Black Metropolis*, 673–79.

7. Melvin D. Williams, *Community in a Black Pentecostal Church: An Anthropological Study* (Pittsburgh: University of Pittsburgh Press, 1974); Benton Johnson, "Do Holiness Sects Socialize in Dominant Values?" *Social Forces* 39 (May 1961): 309–16; Joseph R. Washington, Jr., *Black Sects and Cults: The Power Axis in an Ethnic Ethic* (New York: Doubleday, 1972); Paul Oliver, *Songsters and Saints: Vocal Traditions on Race Records* (New York: Cambridge University Press, 1984), 169–98.

8. Mays and Nicholson, *The Negro's Church*, 224–27; Welty, "Black Shepherds," 243–44, 300–11. See also Spurgeon E. Crayton, "The His-

tory of the National Fraternal Council of Negro Churches" (M.A. thesis, Union Theological Seminary, New York, 1979).

9. Howard M. Brotz, *The Black Jews of Harlem: Negro Nationalism and the Dilemmas of Negro Leadership* (New York: Schocken, 1964); Deanne Shapiro, "Double Damnation, Double Salvation: The Sources and Varieties of Black Judaism in the United States" (M.A. thesis, Columbia University, 1970).

10. Fauset, *Black Gods*, 41–51.

11. C. Eric Lincoln, *The Black Muslims in America* (Boston: Beacon Press, 1961); E. U. Essien-Udom, *Black Nationalism: A Search for Identity in America* (Chicago: University of Chicago Press, 1962).

12. Merril Charles Singer, "Saints of the Kingdom: Group Emergence, Individual Affiliation, and Social Change among the Black Hebrews of Israel" (Ph.D. diss., University of Utah, 1979); Ben Ammi, *God, the Black Man, and Truth* (Chicago: Communicators Press, 1982).

13. Yvonne Yazbeck Haddad, "Muslims in the United States," in *Islam: The Religious and Political Life of a World Community*, ed. Marjorie Kelly (New York: Praeger, 1984), 265–71.

14. Gayraud S. Wilmore and James H. Cone, eds., *Black Theology: A Documentary History, 1966–1979* (Maryknoll, N.Y.: Orbis Books, 1979), 15–111.

21. Ibid., 609–23.

22. Leon H. Sullivan, *Build Brother Build* (Philadelphia: Macrae, 1969).

CHAPTER SIX. MINORITY WITHIN A MINORITY

1. John Carroll, "Report for the Eminent Cardinal Antonelli Concerning the State of Religion in the United States of America" (1785); reprinted in John Tracy Ellis, ed., *Documents of American Catholic History*, 3 vols. (Wilmington, Del.: Michael Glazier, 1987), 1: 148–49. A book-length survey of the history of black Catholics has appeared since this essay was written: Cyprian Davis, *The History of Black Catholics in the United States* (New York: Crossroad, 1990).

2. Lyle Saxon, Robert Tallant, and Edward Dreyer, eds., *Gumbo Ya-Ya: A Collection of Louisiana Folk Tales* (New York: Bonanza Books, 1945), 242; Frederick Law Olmsted, *The Cotton Kingdom*, 2 vols. (New York, 1861), 2: 35–36.

3. Pierre Landry, "From Slavery to Freedom," unpublished memoirs, cited by Charles Bathelemy Rousseve, *The Negro in Louisiana* (New Orleans: Xavier University Press, 1937), 39.

4. Father James Joubert, "The Original Diary of the Oblate Sisters of Providence, 1827–42," Oblate Sisters of Providence Archives, Baltimore, 12; cited by Sister Mary of Good Counsel Baptiste, "A Study of the Foundation and Educational Objectives of the Congregation of the Oblate Sisters of Providence and of the Achievement of These Objectives as Seen in Their Schools" (M.A. thesis, Villanova University, Department of Education, 1939), 24.

5. Letter of Father Charles Nerinckx, May 1824, cited in Anna C. Minogue, *Loretto: Annals of the Century* (New York: America Press, 1912), 96.

6. Patrick Healy to Father George Fenwick, November 23, 1853, cited in Albert S. Foley, S.J., *God's Men of Color: The Colored Catholic Priests of the United States, 1854–1954* (New York: Farrar, Straus, 1955), 25; Bishop Fitzpatrick to Archbishop Hughes, July 10, 1859, cited in ibid., 15.

7. Slattery's sermon was printed under the title *Rev. John Henry Dorsey, A Colored Man, Was Ordained Priest by His Eminence, Cardinal Gibbons in Baltimore Cathedral, June Twenty-First, 1902* (privately printed, n.p., n.d.), 9–10, John H. Dorsey file, Josephite Fathers Archives, Baltimore, Md. See Stephen J. Ochs's important study of black Catholic priests, *Desegregating the Altar: The Josephites and the Struggle for Black Priests, 1871–1960* (Baton Rouge: Louisiana State University Press, 1990).

8. John J. Plantevigne to Archbishop James H. Blenk, March 23, 1909, John J. Plantevigne file, Josephite Fathers Archives.

9. Archbishop James H. Blenk to John J. Plantevigne, March 31, 1909, and John J. Plantevigne to Archbishop James H. Blenk, April 13, 1909, John J. Plantevigne file, Josephite Fathers Archives.

10. Cited in Foley, *God's Men of Color*, 89–90.

11. *Three Catholic Afro-American Congresses* (Cincinnati: American Catholic Tribune, 1893; reprint, New York: Arno Press, 1878), 141–142.

12. Marilyn Wenzke Nickels, "The Federated Colored Catholics: A Study of Three Variant Perspectives on Racial Justice as Represented by John LaFarge, William Markoe, and Thomas Turner" (Ph.D. diss., Catholic University of America, 1975), 37–38; published as *Black Catholic Protest and the Federated Colored Catholics, 1917–1933: Three Perspectives on Racial Justice* (New York: Garland Publishing, 1988).

13. Shane Leslie, ed., *Letters of Herbert Cardinal Vaughan to Lady Herbert of Lea, 1867 to 1903* (London: Burns, Oates, 1942), 240.

14. "A Statement of the Black Catholic Clergy Caucus, April 18, 1968," reprinted in Gayraud Wilmore and James Cone, eds., *Black Theology: A Documentary History*, 2 vols., 2d ed., rev. (Maryknoll, N.Y.: Orbis Books, 1993), 1:230.

CHAPTER SEVEN. THE CHANTED SERMON

1. Given its importance in African-American culture, the literature on the "folk," or chanted, sermon is not as extensive as one might suppose. The following works have heavily influenced my treatment: James Weldon Johnson, *God's Trombones: Seven Negro Sermons in Verse* (New York: Viking Press, 1927); William H. Pipes, *Say Amen, Brother! Old-Time Negro Preaching: A Study in American Frustration* (New York: William Frederick Press, 1951); Bruce A. Rosenberg, *The Art of the American Folk Preacher* (New York: Oxford University Press, 1970), "The Psychology of the Spiritual Sermon," in *Religious Movements in Contemporary America*, ed. Irving I. Zaretsky and Mark P. Leone (Princeton: Princeton University Press, 1974), 13–49; Henry H. Mitchell, *Black Preaching* (Philadelphia: J. B. Lippincott, 1970); Gerald L. Davis, *I Got the Word in Me and I Can Sing It, You Know: A Study of the Performed African-American Sermon* (Philadelphia: University of Pennsylvania Press, 1985).

2. See Paul Laurence Dunbar's poem, "An Antebellum Sermon," most

easily accessible in Dudley Randall, ed., *The Black Poets* (New York: Bantam Books, 1971), 44–46; Johnson, *God's Trombones*; Ralph Ellison, *Invisible Man* (New York: Signet Books, 1952), 12–13; William Faulkner, *The Sound and the Fury* (New York: Vintage Books, 1946), 356–71; Paule Marshall, *Praisesong for the Widow* (New York: E. P. Dutton, 1983), 198–203. The speeches of Martin Luther King, Jr., have made this tradition at least vaguely familiar to many Americans otherwise unacquainted with it. Although male-dominated, the tradition has also been exemplified by women preachers who usually had to struggle against clerical resistance to exercise their talents to preach.

3. I urge the reader to listen to a recording or radio broadcast of a chanted sermon, or better yet, visit a church in which this type of preaching is performed. The Reverend C. L. Franklin, father of Aretha, has recorded more than seventy albums of sermons on Chess and Jewel labels. See Jeff Todd Titon, ed., *Give Me This Mountain: Reverend C. L. Franklin, Life History and Selected Sermons* (Urbana: University of Illinois Press, 1989). Sunday evening broadcasts of black church services are common. The chanted sermon *must be heard* to be understood.

4. Rosenberg, *Art of the American Folk Preacher*, 48.

5. Rosenberg's description of the use of formulas in oral composition differs from Lord's: Lord thought that "new formulas" were created by analogy with the old, the composition process [being] merely one of substituting a word or phrase." Rosenberg, applying the insights of generative theory, suggests that the preacher "has at his command . . . not several score or several hundred formulas which he manipulates by word and phrase substitution, but rather a metrical deep structure which enables him to generate an infinite number of sentences in his native meter." Note these positions are not mutually exclusive. See Rosenberg, "Psychology of the Spiritual Sermon," 141, and *Art of the American Folk Preacher*, 46–116; Pipes, *Say Amen, Brother!* 150–55.

6. Frederick Law Olmsted, *The Cotton Kingdom*, 2 vols. (New York, 1861).

7. Mary Boykin Chestnut, *A Diary from Dixie*, ed. Ben Ames Williams (Boston: Houghton Mifflin, 1949), 148–49.

8. For fuller treatment of African influence upon the religious worship of American slaves, see Albert J. Raboteau, *Slave Religion: The "Invisible Institution" in the Antebellum South* (New York: Oxford University Press: 1978), 48–75.

9. Morton Marks, "Uncovering Ritual Structures in Afro-American Music," in Zaretsky and Leone, *Religious Movements in Contemporary America*, 60–134.

10. Clifton H. Johnson, ed., *God Struck Me Dead: Religious Conversion Experiences and Autobiographies of Ex-slaves* (Philadelphia: Pilgrim Press, 1969), 144.

CHAPTER EIGHT. THE CONVERSION EXPERIENCE

1. Charles Stearn, *Narrative of Henry Box Brown* (Boston, 1849), 17–18.

2. Author's interviews with elderly black residents of Mt. Pleasant, S.C., John's Island, S.C., Sunbury, Ga., and Sapelo Island, Ga., in 1985–86.

3. James Baldwin, *Go Tell It on the Mountain* (1952; reprint, New York: Dell Publishing; 1985), 27–28.

4. Ibid., 23–24.

5. Ibid., 200.

6. Ibid., 200–201.

7. Ibid., 202–4.

8. Ibid., 204–5.

9. James Baldwin, *The Fire Next Time* (1963; reprint, New York: Random House, Vintage International, 1993), 98–99.

CHAPTER NINE. A HIDDEN WHOLENESS

1. Merton discussed the planned retreat in correspondence with June and John Yungblut in January and February of 1968. See William H. Shannon, ed., *The Hidden Ground of Love: The Letters of Thomas Merton on Religious Experience and Social Concerns* (New York: Farrar, Straus, Giroux, 1985), 639–41, 644.

2. For details of Merton's life, see his autobiography, *The Seven Storey Mountain* (New York: Harcourt Brace Jovanovich, 1948), and the most complete biography, Michael Mott's *The Seven Mountains of Thomas Merton* (Boston: Houghton Mifflin, 1984).

3. The biographies of King I have found most useful are David Levering Lewis, *King: A Biography*, 2d ed. (Urbana: University of Illinois Press, 1978); Stephen B. Oates, *Let the Trumpet Sound: The Life of Martin Luther King, Jr.* (New York: Harper and Row, 1982); and David J. Garrow, *Bearing the Cross: Martin Luther King, Jr., and the Southern Christian Leadership Conference* (New York: William Morrow, 1986). John J. Ansbro, *Martin Luther King, Jr.: The Making of a Mind* (Maryknoll, N.Y.: Orbis Books, 1982), is a helpful analysis of King's thought. James M. Washington has edited a fine collection of King's sermons, speeches, and addresses, *A Testament of Hope: The Essential Writings of Martin Luther King, Jr.* (San Francisco: Harper and Row, 1986).

4. Martin Luther King, Sr., with Clayton Riley, *Daddy King: An Autobiography* (New York: William Morrow, 1980), 84–87, 95–102. See also Taylor Branch, *Parting the Waters: America in the King Years* (New York: Simon and Schuster, 1988).

5. Thomas Merton, *Seeds of Destruction* (New York: Farrar, Straus and Giroux, 1964), xiii.

6. Thomas Merton, *Conjectures of a Guilty Bystander* (Garden City, N.Y.: Doubleday, 1966), 140–41. Walnut has since been renamed Muhammed Ali after one of Louisville's more notable native sons.

7. Merton, *Conjectures*, 142.

8. Martin Luther King, Jr., *Stride toward Freedom: The Montgomery Story* (New York: Harper and Row, 1958), 101.

9. Quoted by Garrow, *Bearing the Cross*, 58. It is significant that King's words "He promised never to leave me, no never leave me alone" echo the words of an old Evangelical hymn, suggesting the importance of tradition in this intensely personal conversion experience.

10. Thomas Merton, *Faith and Violence: Christian Teaching and Christian Practice* (Notre Dame: University of Notre Dame Press, 1968), 130–31.

11. From an address delivered by King in 1962, reprinted in Washington, *Testament of Hope*, 117.

12. Merton, *Seeds of Destruction*, 69; King, *Stride toward Freedom*, 63, 224.

13. King, *Stride toward Freedom*, 101–7.

14. Thomas Merton, "A Tribute to Gandhi," originally published in 1962, reprinted in *Thomas Merton on Peace* (New York: McCall, 1975), 178–79.

15. Merton, *Thomas Merton on Peace*, 211.

16. In his famous "Beyond Vietnam" address, delivered in Riverside Church in 1967, reprinted in Washington, *Testament of Hope*, 240.

17. Thomas Merton, *Raids on the Unspeakable* (New York: New Directions, 1966), 15–16.

18. Merton, *Seeds of Destruction*, 25.

19. Merton, *Raids on the Unspeakable*, 15.

20. Thomas Merton, *Contemplation in a World of Action* (Garden City, N.Y.: Doubleday, 1971), 161.

21. Merton, *Conjectures*, 142. Merton seems to have gotten the term from Louis Massignon, the French scholar of Islam.

22. Ibid.

23. Merton, *Raids on the Unspeakable*, 17–18.

24. Merton, *Contemplation in a World of Action*, 155–56.

25. Christmas sermon 1967, reprinted in Washington, *Testament of Hope*, 255.

26. From a 1962 address, reprinted in ibid., 119.

27. From an article published in *Christian Century*, February 6, 1957, reprinted in ibid., 8–9.

28. From a 1956 sermon and the "Beyond Vietnam" speech, reprinted in ibid., 11, 242.

29. Ibid., 20.

30. Ibid., 254.

EPILOGUE

1. Clifton H. Johnson, ed., *God Struck Me Dead: Religious Conversion Experiences and Autobiographies of Ex-Slaves* (Philadelphia: Pilgrim Press, 1969), 74.

2. Appeal to Governor Thomas Gage and the Massachusetts General Court, May 25, 1774, *Collections of the Massachusetts Historical Society*, 5th ser., 3 (1877): 432–33.

3. Johnson, *God Struck Me Dead*, 144.

—

Index

LaVergne, TN USA
10 December 2009
166630LV00002B/100/P